Water in the Wastelands

Cowley Publications is a ministry of the Society of Saint John the Evangelist, a religious community of men in the Episcopal Church. Emerging from the Society's tradition of prayer, theological reflection, and diversity of mission, the press is centered in the rich heritage of the Anglican Communion.

Cowley Publications seeks to provide books, audio cassettes, CDs, and other resources for the ongoing theological exploration and spiritual development of the Episcopal Church and others in the body of Christ. To this end, it is dedicated to developing a new generation of theological writers, encouraging them to produce timely, creative, and stimulating publications of excellence, and making these publications available widely, reaching both clergy and lay persons.

Water in the Wastelands

the sacrament
of shared suffering

William Blaine-Wallace

Cowley Publications
Cambridge, Massachusetts

Published in the United States of America by Cowley Publications, a division of the Society of Saint John the Evangelist. No portion of this book may be reproduced, stored in or introduced into a retrieval system, or transmitted, in any form or by any means—including photocopying—without the prior written permission of Cowley Publications, except in the case of brief quotations embedded in critical articles and reviews.

Library of Congress Cataloging-in-Publication Data:
Blaine-Wallace, William, 1951-
    Water in the wastelands : the sacrament of shared suffering / William Blaine-Wallace.
        p. cm.
    ISBN 1-56101-209-2 (pbk. : alk. paper)
    1. Consolation. 2. Bereavement—Religious aspects—Episcopal Church—Meditations. 3. Suffering—Religious aspects—Episcopal Church—Meditations. 4. Death—Religious aspects—Episcopal Church—Meditations. I. Title.
    BV4905.3 .B53 2002
    242'.4—dc21

                                    2002154276

Scripture quotations are taken from The New Revised Standard Version of the Bible, © 1989, by the Division of Christian Education of the National Council of the Churches of Christ in the United States of America. Used by permission.

Cover art: Crucifix, 1999: Jae Hee Hur. Oil on canvas. Used by permission.
Cover design: Jennifer Hopcroft

This book was printed in the United States of America on acid-free paper.

Cowley Publications
907 Massachusetts Avenue
Cambridge, Massachusetts 02139
800-225-1534 · www.cowley.org

The violets in the mountains have broken the rocks.

Tennessee Williams

Contents

Acknowledgments

A mother, whose daughter died at the age of twelve, said that for the longest time she felt enveloped in a thick fog of numbness, despair, anger and sadness. Yet, through the march of years in the company of family and friends, the fog slowly lifted. What remains are memories, which can be touched now and then over the span of a day: "I gently tap my chest, just over the heart, and remember. Sometimes I smile. Sometimes I cry."

This book is a similar tapping of the chest. After spending many years among the dying and bereaved as counselor and companion, clarity slowly emerges that enables veiled articulation, here and there, of a grace at the center of the community of bent and broken people, what Flannery O'Conner called the "image at the heart of things."

Any accounting of my articulations conjures up big company. I am thankful for, and forever blessed by, the space given fellow caregivers and me in the lives of the few thousand folks who died on our watch, and those who love them. I greatly appreciate the gentle and wise titration of insight, direction, and engagement given by my Cowley editors, Kevin Hackett SSJE and Ulrike Guthrie. I treasure the parish I serve, Emmanuel

Church, Boston, a community that desires and demands story in, under, around and through the sermonic task. I thank Emmanuel Church, also, for the generous sabbatical, during which this book was written. I am grateful to J.S. Bach, whose cantatas 2, 20, 21, 39, 82, 99, 106 and 199 kept me company during the writing. And, Beethoven's late string quartet, opus 132, the third movement, which "pulled up a chair" during the final edit (I've heard that Beethoven's tear stains are on the original manuscript.). I am honored to have a "jury" of friends and colleagues whose sometimes real, other times imagined spirit stood over my shoulder as I prayed this project to paper: Victoria Blaine-Wallace, Betsy Bunn, Suzanne Colburn, Carter Heyward, Russell Holmes, Sarah Lawrence Lightfoot, Patricia Long, Michael Shea, Paul Solman, Paula Lawrence Wehmiller, my spiritual director colleagues group at Bethany House of Prayer, and members of the Hanover Trust.

I am most grateful for, and graced by, family. Their closeness and care over the years and during the course of writing deepened my capacity and courage to remember well. Thank you Victoria, Jennifer, Sarah Frances, and Julian.

Introduction
A Plentiful Path to the Place of the Skull

When Jesus saw his mother and the disciple whom he
loved standing beside her, he said to his mother,
"Woman, here is your son." Then he said to the disciple,
"Here is your mother." And from that hour the disciple
took her into his own home.   John 19:25b-27

J esus died a shameful and cruel death, outside the walls
of religious and political conventions, with only a handful of followers near him—his mother and beloved disciple, an aunt and a cherished friend. The words and actions of Jesus about the home his mother and beloved
disciple would make after his death mirror the relations
he established with the ill-regarded and disregarded folks
that he encountered on the journey to Golgotha. Jesus
died the way he lived.

In the initial decade of the AIDS pandemic, people
who died from AIDS in America, and those who loved
them, experienced a passion similar to Jesus and his long

time companions—shame, cruelty, church and state rejection, abandonment. The words and actions shared on the way towards and at their deathbeds often echoed those of Jesus on the way toward and at his execution. The community of AIDS both created new and jury-rigged existing ways to care for and commune with the ostracized, overlooked and overburdened ones.

Jonathan was in the last days of his dying at the AIDS hospice. His lover, Ken, had been at his side throughout the previous weeks, having taken time away from his job as a buyer of designer clothing for a chain of high-end department stores. Jonathan's parents, farmers from rural Maine, far removed by values and lifestyle from the experiences of urban life, homosexuality, gay relationships, and dying centers, came to see their son before he died. A nervous dad in bib overalls and a now tentative Ken faced each other across Jonathan's bed. After what seemed like an eternity of awkward silence, they simultaneously reached across the bed, embraced, and cried in each other's arms. Jonathan placed a hand on each of their backs.

The path to the place of the skull, for Jesus and his friends and people with AIDS and their friends, is a plentiful one. The solidarity that springs from the soil of their shared suffering reaps a rich harvest of abundant joy. It's what the apostle Paul called "the peace that passes understanding." The peace that emanates from their shared suffering is different from happiness, contentment, or satisfaction. This peace purrs. Their peace is the counterpoint of conviviality.

Jesus and his disciples multiply meager food to feed thousands of hungry people. A small consortium of Boston activists, physicians, health care administrators, and politicians instigate an initiative to acquire expensive and vital prescription drugs for persons with AIDS who fall through the cracks of private health insurance and government reimbursement programs.

Jesus descends the mountain of Transfiguration and immediately heals a young man possessed with demons. The clinical director of the AIDS hospice sneaks away from the resident-staff Halloween party to be at the bedside of Valerie as she dies.

Jesus and his followers enter Jerusalem before a crowd waving palm branches and shouting various and sundry hosannas. Strong and flamboyant David, not yet physically compromised by AIDS, pushes AIDS-ravaged Donald in his wheelchair along the Gay Pride Parade route, under the banner of The Hospice at Mission Hill. The shouts and cheers of the already jubilant crowd soar as David and Donald pass by.

Mary washes Jesus' feet with her tears, anoints him with costly ointment in preparation for burial. The hospice social worker helps Thomas, a carpenter, sand the extravagant casket he has carved for his burial.

The plentiful path to the place of the skull is not only found in the wilderness experience of severely wounded people. It also cuts across the map of our relatively ordered lives. The hindsight of our histories reveals that much of our peace has been honed on the subtle, serpentine side road of our shared suffering, a road which we would unlikely have selected as a road to spiritual wellness. Part of our spiritual quest is to make hindsight about the fecundity of our shared suffering foresight. One aspect of our calling is to live in a manner that expresses the gospel truth about the fruitfulness of collective frailty.

Fashioning such foresight involves more than calculating how we might make our way through future episodes of life-limiting illness and loss. We may step on the plentiful path to the place of the skull right now.

The course of our present lives is different from that of dying and mourning persons in that the majority of us are not facing a terminal illness or death of a loved one. Yet, the difference between the little girl in bed two of room eight on the cancer unit and us, who are wondering what we might do this weekend, is one of degree rather than kind. For our lives are daily fraught with the little and not-so-little deaths and bereavements that loom large. We, too, are acquainted with grief occasioned by illness, dark nights of the soul, bent and broken relationships.

Take my life over the last couple of days. I stole away to Maine to do some spirited writing and the solitude was soiled by dispiritedness. My deadness was occasioned by inattention to prayer over the last several weeks, due to around-the-clock demands to which I had given unwarranted allegiance.

An elderly friend's fear of serious surgery was not helped by the fact that his children did not take time from their busy lives to show up at his side. He asked me to hold his hand until it was time for him to go through the stainless steel swinging doors.

I had dinner with a friend who is losing muscle mass in his legs for some unknown reason. His livelihood, not to mention a good slice of his sense of self, ride on those legs.

Tomorrow I preside at the committal service of my wife's aunt, who had been a precious presence in her life, especially during difficult times. The service falls on the anniversary of the death of my wife's first husband.

I'm betting that your lives haven't been much different from mine. All of us walk through "the valley of the shadow" — the shadow! — "of death."

My intent is not to honor or glorify suffering. Suffering is suffering. Gary would trade all the wisdom he gained through grieving Robert's death for one more Saturday morning together with tea, croissants, and *The Times*. Rather, I am cheering the resonance and resilience of the human spirit that oozes from the web of suffering persons, who, finding that they are more like than unlike one another, risk less-defended, more empathic and connected hearts. Interdependent hearts heal and are healed.

In the following meditations, sacred wisdom is secreted from mundane stories about shared suffering. Such wisdom encourages us not to so quickly avoid or leap off our plentiful paths to the place of the skull. Even though the mundane stories are of those sharing a suffering which is probably more intense or insidious than ours, the sacred wisdom imparted does pertain to us, people who seek to live a life of integrity and meaning amidst the daily vicissitudes of an ephemeral existence.

In the Christian experience, the amalgam of the sacred and mundane makes for sacrament. "Sacraments," as my seminary preaching professor said, "are heavenly manna in earthen vessels." Sometimes such a fusion is manifest beyond the likes of Body/bread, Blood/wine. Now and then, our lives in relation strike a chord so elemental as to ring of the eternal.[1] The sacramental sound communicates dimensions of the heart of God previously outside the purview of our conscious prayerfulness. These are grace notes.

The music of grace most often heard through these sacramental stories pertains to a paradoxical power—the power inherent in vulnerabilities faced, fashioned, and forestalled through shared suffering. This power is dif-

---

1. In the Catechism of *The Book of Common Prayer*, under the heading, "Other Sacramental Rites," page 861, sacraments are said to be "patterns of countless ways by which God uses material things to reach out to us."

ferent than power as generally understood. Conventional wisdom defines power as that which defends, sets apart, and moves towards invincibility.

The ironic power of these stories breaks upon us as an upside-down, unsettling grace. It neuters the fashionable conventions by which we are accustomed to living our lives as the sufficient inhabitants of the first among First World nations. Such grace cracks us open to the emptiness of an aeon of thinly veneered adequacy, and gives us chance after chance to join a band of itinerant and alien souls making their way down a dusty road as a regiment of wounded healers in heaven's reign.

The habit of living formed by the following stories suggests that the power of vulnerability offers us, citizens of the dominant/dominating nation, a good chance to prosper our primary and public relations towards the redemption of a broken world and the reconciliation of estranged peoples. My prayer is that you, the reader of these sacraments of shared suffering, may experience "grace upon grace" as you relate to yourself and your neighbors near and far.

1 ❧

A Proximate Heaven

The time is fulfilled, and the kingdom of
God has come near.   Mark 1:15

Last year, I was on silent retreat at Christ in the Desert monastery in northern New Mexico. I took the retreat two months before my wedding. My intent was to climb the tallest tree of prayerfulness I could find before making a second marriage. From there, I would look back over the rugged and winding trail of my past, look forward towards the extraordinary promise of the future, and integrate the landscapes into a meaningful whole. After a couple of days of prayerfulness in that tree, I discovered that the Divine Presence is afraid of heights and leery of lofty agendas.

At Christ in the Desert, there are two degrees of silence. There is qualified silence. Guests and monks talk at appointed times and places. Those who desire absolute silence wear a symbol around their necks indicating a request not to be engaged. I chose the former.

One morning, while defrosting a freezer during work

hours, one of the brothers asked if I had connected with the other two guests from the Carolinas, my roots. I sought them out after lunch, expecting that they would not have chosen absolute silence. They had not.

What followed was a serendipitous encounter between three fellows from very similar backgrounds and with quite the same intentions for their retreats. They, too, had come to climb the tallest tree in the forest of their prayerfulness in order to look backward, forward, with hope for some melding of the two.

One had reached a pinnacle in his career as an investment banker. The air up top was thinner than he had expected. He took six weeks off to assess his life, dissect the ruckus his brooding was causing in his marriage and with his employees, and prospect for a new beginning. The other recently had retired from human resources administration. His curiosity about meditation and spirituality led him to the desert among religious to discern what the future might hold for him.

We developed fast friendships that were celebrated at "happy hour" each evening at sunset. We conceded that the better part of our prayerfulness was practiced in immediate community rather than prayerful perches from which we hoped to see where we had been and where we might go. We acknowledged that our community at day's end sharpened our attention to the stillness around us, gave greater meaning to our times of silence, and heightened our participation in liturgy. We came to better understand the convivial core from which sagacious solitude springs.

During one of our conversations, the retiree shared a story from the literature of the fourth century desert mothers and fathers that captured the heart of our concession to the relational moment as the thinnest membrane between the holy and us. A merchant from the city sought out a desert father to find solace strong enough to ease the anxiety of his life. The man conveyed to the desert father where he had been with his life and where he might go. A few minutes into the merchant's agitated ranting, the desert father interrupted and said, "If you have one foot in the past and the other in the future, you're pissing on the present."

Three fellows retreated to the desert to discover that the vastness of one's life is just too much for one soul to get her or his arms around at any given time, even with God's help! The immensity of one's life is best cradled, and a tad comprehended, in the company of others in the present moment. The weight of an ambiguous existence dodges final definition and integration. Company bears it. From the company of unclear and uncertain people comes courage to carry on as those graced enough to see through the glass dimly.

Whether in downtown Atlanta or rural Vermont, dying and bereaved people readily make the kind of company my friends and I unexpectedly found in alien wilderness. A middle-aged woman in the last stages of lung cancer, who gets transfused not for cure's sake, but for the added energy needed to eat supper with her husband and children, does not have to go to New Mexico for desert wisdom. The demands and challenges occasioned by terminal illness and loss either cloud or make pointless the human quest to find a seam stitch of meaning running through the fabric of an expansive life. Dying and bereaved people try to keep the seam stitch of what increasingly becomes each expansive day from ripping loose. They put the darning needle to the fabric of immediate relations.

I asked a young man dying with AIDS to tell me the hardest thing about his dying. He paused for several seconds and then said, "I go out with my best friends every

Friday night. We've been doing it for years. Now they make it hard for me to take my turn paying the bill."

And then there is Christopher, our parish administrator, who died from AIDS after being relatively symptom free for twelve years. I had a what-do-I-want-to-do-when-I-grow-up conversation with him one afternoon in his office. I shared my ambivalence about accepting the call to Emmanuel as the elected rector. For the past two years, I had served as the appointed vicar.

After listening to the noise of my angst, Christopher said, "One thing I like about having a terminal illness is that I do not have to worry about what I am going to do with my life. Instead, I am left to ask myself each day how I might, in the company of others, bless God." Christopher, on many occasions, was my desert father, who kept me from pissing on the present.

Dying and bereaved persons are better able to see heaven's immediacy. They are strong and agile enough in their weakness to pick up heaven now. They are wise enough to sense that the heaven they hold or, better yet, the heaven that holds them, are moments of mutual relation through which eternal life flows.

I recall a letter to a mother from her dying son. The mother was worried that her son's homosexuality would bar him from heaven. The son wrote to his mother that she should not worry about whether heaven would be his reward since eternal life was what he was experiencing now in the community formed through his illness.

Granted, there is immensely more to heaven than that which is embodied in the relational moment. And, unfortunately, the endless acres of heaven that are beyond instances of mutual relation capture most of our attention on any given day. On an ordinary Tuesday morning, from the lofty perches of an inescapable ache for a meaningful life amidst the messiness of living, we will fling cosmic questions: Where have I been? Where am I going? What am I to do? What matters? What finally matters? We are like Elijah running from Jezebel, fleeing up Mount Horeb, where God had shown up before, to get a Word, any word. The vast majority of the time, we, like Elijah, will hear a "still small voice." Hebrew is helpful here: Not a peep.

My prayer is that a fortuitous Wind will shake our trees, sending us back to earth, where we will discover, again, the Eternal's propensity for interim answers, like the one given by Mary Oliver, in the poem, *Wild Geese*: "Tell me about despair, yours, and I will tell you mine." Or about desire, sadness, delight, remorse.

In the meantime, between our dubious ascents, dying and bereaved people remind us of heaven's proximate acre. Elizabeth Barrett Browning expresses their astuteness: "Earth's crammed with heaven and every bush afire with God. Those who see take off their shoes. The rest sit round and pluck blackberries."

2 ∝

The Energy of
Insufficiency

*God said to the rich man, "Fool! This very night life is
being demanded of you; and the things you have prepared, whose will they be?" So it is with those who store
up treasures for themselves but are not rich toward God.*

Luke 12:16-20

Following September 11th, a short but shrill nationwide
debate ensued regarding a national identification card.
Many countries have national ID cards as a way to en-
hance security, particularly in respect to terrorism. Pro-
ponents claim that it's time to join the rest of the world in
terms of the pervasive threat of terror. Opponents assert
an assault upon individual rights. The most strident foes
announce another piece of evidence that gov'ment aims
to eviscerate the particularly American virtues of personal autonomy and self-actualization.

Individual autonomy and actualization are mainly
American temperaments. We have internalized our Euro-

centric origins of colonial dominance and the pioneer ethos of our beginnings to fashion a frontier spirit that is manifested as much in Manhattan as Montana. Our souls are seduced from a variety of sources to surrender to an underlying aim of life: move up and out however, whenever, wherever. Our icon is the *Marlboro Man*, who exudes a rugged and unruly distinctiveness. Our intonation is one of unbounded possibility—*Just Do It*. The spirit of individual autonomy and actualization is pervasive.

Our nation is slowly waking up to the exorbitant cost to community caused by the autonomy and actualization of the self. We are being roused by a growing awareness, thanks to the likes of Enron and WorldCom, that greed is the granddaddy of individual autonomy and actualization. Some voices have heralded the harm of a politic of personal autonomy and actualization long before Kenneth Lay and his lieutenants were in the looting business. In religious circles, the strongest voices are those of the interfaith liberation, feminist, womanist, and queer movements. These voices want us to hear four things more clearly.

First, the evolution of self has been at the expense of others, particularly those who are not straight, white, adult, and male. Many are co-opted or cast aside in the self's quest for autonomy and actualization.

Second, there no longer is enough room for the evolution of individual selves. There is little "West" left towards which one—one person, one class, one gender, one nation—can head. Figuratively speaking, what used to be the Promised Land beyond the Mississippi are now the deep waters of the Pacific...where sharks lurk. Our neighbors—neighbors being the person "next door" or the nation "across the street"—are tired of being either moved or stepped over.

Third, the largest and loudest collective of autonomous

and actualized selves, our nation, does not necessarily know what's best for the rest of the world. Gandhi and Nelson Mandela remind us of, and most nations are signaling their impatience with, the diseased heart of imperialistic presumptuousness. First, second and third world nations are on to our "Father Knows Best" beneficence. They catch on that father knows what's best for father.

Fourth, the innocent hope of the privileged sector of our citizenry for a life of almost limitless possibility is an illusion. The prospect of dirty bombs detonated over Chicago remind us that the noise of explosions, the sight of senseless death, the sense of lurking danger are no longer "over there." For America, as it has been for the most of the rest of the world much of the time, the sweet, eschatological dream of an interdependent world to come is becoming the apocalyptic option for a present world teetering on the edge of destruction. What was a nice lyric by Barbara Streisand, "People who need people are the luckiest people in the world," is now a salient strategy for salvation this side of the by and by.

Antagonists of the American dream, within the Christian tradition, footnote their faith claims through a focus on the fellowship of Jesus before the conversion of Emperor Constantine in the fourth century. Since the time that the emperor converted to Christianity through the witness of Augustine's mother, the church more often than not has been the loudspeaker for the cultural idealism of dominant nations.

The virtues of personal autonomy and actualization did not cross the screen of brother Jesus and his band of followers, and was hardly more than a hiccup in the pre-Constantine church. When scripture is seen without the "corrective lens" of the dominant culture, there emerges an encompassing orientation and sacred allegiance to the antithesis of our cultural icon of self-sufficiency—insufficiency. The gospel witnesses to a gathering of deficient ones, whose sufficiency was plied from an interdependent pooling of a meager amount of things material.

In Matthew's account of Jesus' call and commissioning of the twelve disciples (10:7-13), there is thick connection between the disciples' power to heal and an insufficiency that placed them in a susceptible position to neighbor; so susceptible that they were warned to move on when the neighbor would not share the peculiar peace of powerlessness. Warned to move on, but not to shed their vulnerability:

> And preach as you go, saying, "The kingdom of heaven is near." Heal the sick, raise the dead, cleanse lepers, cast out demons. You received without pay, give without pay. Take no gold, nor silver, nor copper in your belts, no bag for your journey, nor two tunics, nor sandals, nor a staff; for the laborer deserves his food. And whatever town or village you enter, find out who is worthy in it, and stay with him until you depart. As you enter the house, salute it. And if the house is worthy, let your peace come upon it; but if it is not worthy, let your peace return to you.

The American church has a hard time mimicking biblical insufficiency, and not just because we like our toys. Our more than half-century honeymoon with things therapeutic causes us to readily misinterpret insufficiency, both its nature and cure.

Insufficiency is usually preached from the pulpit and perceived in the pews as having to do with shame, whom a person is not. To the shortness of self, the "relevant" church responds with the salvo of whom someone is in the eyes of God. Being beloved and valued by God overcomes one's sense of inadequacy. The restoration of our adequacy Sunday by Sunday enables us to continue Monday by Monday the quest for greater autonomy and actualization. In terms of the psychology of self, and the disease and cure of self, there is not that much difference between Robert Schuller's Sunday morning sermons from The Crystal Cathedral about "being somebody," widely ridiculed in theologically liberal circles, and Paul Tillich's famous, five decade old meditation in a progressive university chapel entitled, "You are Accepted."

Surprise! The community of the dying and bereaved, the community the church has ministered to for two millennia, now comes to *our* bedside. This community mirrors biblical insufficiency for a sickly sufficient culture and her mostly domesticated religious life.

Insufficiency in the community of the dying and bereaved is pedestrian. I mean pedestrian in a literal sense. For dying and bereaved persons, insufficiency's nature and cure has more to do with the task of walking through day-to-day life in relation rather than with one's psychological or spiritual "state of being."

Relatively hale and hearty people have been exiled, by disease and loss, from the nation of their sufficiency to the foreign soil of insufficiency. There they eventually find other exiles and discover surprising strength in their collective weakness. Community is established within the perimeters of shared insufficiency.

Insufficiency's nature is more about failure to thrive in the moment than shame regarding one's essence. Cure is less about overcoming insufficiency by means of a new understanding of one's worth and more about having one's insufficiency contained in a context beyond self.

When I was executive director of a health care organization that operated an AIDS hospice, I occasionally served as a nurse's assistant to soften my CEO status. The morning of my first day, I reported to the nurse's station with high anxiety, which wasn't eased when I was told to give Michael a bed bath. Michael was a resident I had come to know through conversation in the day room. By this time, Michael had wasted away to skin and bone. Furthermore, I had never given an adult male a bath.

After more than a little small talk, I asked Michael if he was ready for his bath. He responded by saying that he was. As I dipped the washcloth in the pale of warm water, thinking that the cloth would initially land on his forehead, Michael just happened to mention that I might feel awkward bathing him. He told me not to worry too much, that he felt at least as awkward having me, a relative stranger, wash his now gaunt and wrinkled self. He said that we would talk our way through it, one step at a time. Off we go. Our mutual weakness at the outset added up to incredible strength at the end.

The extended hand of an emaciated wherewithal is the church's implausible fount of divine energy. Such "outreach" is our essential witness to an autonomous nation that is too actualized for its own good.

3 ❧

The Tie that Binds
and Rebuilds

Blessed are the meek, for they will inherit the earth.

Matthew 5:5

Our AIDS hospice, upon opening, was a showcase. Literally. The finest design firms in the city came together to create an environment that included all the comforts of home and more. Each firm created a space—bedroom, common area, kitchen—that reflected its particular vision and the hospice's general approach to community.

One bedroom had a ceiling that was painted as a sky, complete with puffy clouds on which a sick soul could imagine drifting in security or bliss. Another had a wall painted as a grape vine, inviting occupants to dream of sunning outside in the Tuscan sun. Over the mantle in a living room hung a Mapplethorpe print, intended to give residents a sense of pride in their home and an air of urban elegance.

Before the first person came to die among us, we opened the hospice to the public. It was quite a splash—*Metropolitan Home* and *Architectural Digest* covered our "do."

All the comforts of home and more. Soon, however, we would be reminded that the comforts we had assembled largely reflected the values and tastes of white, middle class, gay men, who were the primary constituents of the visible AIDS community in the 1980's.

The narrowness of our design was exposed when Johnny came to live with us. Johnny was poor, black, addicted, streetwise, and straight. Johnny was a preview of what would become the predominate patient profile of our hospice. He showed us the AIDS devil was becoming less discriminate.

Johnny's adjustment to us was not gentle, nor was the welcome we extended him particularly warm.

Johnny did not know much about art, much less Mapplethorpe. "Fags" freaked him out, as did their tastes. He didn't get our pride in the place. He didn't like the music we listened to, food we ate, movies we watched, or magazines we read. He didn't relate to the families we had or the visitors we received. Johnny stayed to himself and in his room for the first couple of weeks.

We barely tried to coax Johnny out of his funk or space. None of us worked very hard to break the loud silence that hovered over the table during the few times he took his meals in the dining room. The music that blasted from his stereo was a far cry from the lyricism of Patsy Cline or Liza Minelli, and it violated our ears. When we did peak into his room, the posters we glimpsed gave us pause. And Johnny's friends, when they came to see him, seemed to demand a wide path on the way to his room, and we gave it to them.

Ronnie, once a popular drag queen around town,

was the first to cross the cultural threshold that separated Johnny from the rest of us. Ronnie's courage to move off familiar ground, onto the foreign soil that was Johnny's life, radiated from his awareness of one thing he presently shared with Johnny—a virulent bout with *Pneumocystis Carinni*, pneumonia AIDS-style. Ronnie and Johnny shared the bond of breathlessness.

Upon this foundational connection, Ronnie and Johnny built an abiding relationship. Their shared suffering of a disease and its particular symptoms, as well as the marginal position they shared in society (that one was flambouyantly gay and the other poor and black meant that both were located about the same, long distance from power and privilege), were catalysts for a friendship that bridged the chasm of class that separated them. Their differences came to be more incidental than essential.

Ronnie's and Johnny's friendship was contagious. Their hilarity, affection, teasing, and delight spun a web of relation through the hospice that few escaped. That web proved strong enough to support the increasing weight of economic, social, ethnic, racial, and religious diversity within the hospice walls over the next several years.

The bond of breathlessness that was the matrix of Ronnie and Johnny's friendship awakens us, once again, to what I consider to be God's golden rule: the strongest tie that binds one to another is our mutual woe. This tie makes for a rather efficient and effective ecclesiology, which mirrors Will Campbell's definition of church in *Brother to a Dragonfly*: "One cat in one ditch and one nobody of a son of a bitch trying to pull her out."

When our mutual woes are discovered and shared, foreigner becomes friend. When foreigner becomes friend, genuine reconciliation supplants thin détente.

When foreigner becomes friend, the reign of heaven is increased.

Take, for example, the silver lining to the dark, dark cloud of September 11th. Many of us discovered in the swell of compassion for lives lost on that terrible day that the vast majority of Muslims actually are more alike than unlike Christians and Jews. The myth of our radical differences was dispelled by a broad anguish that brought us close enough to clearly see each other again or for the first time. The sacrament of shared suffering offered around the altar of horror was a paragon of cultural, ethnic and religious diversity and closeness. Who knows what long lasting peace initiatives and advances will stem from a few weeks of mutual woe?

The sacrament of shared suffering enables us to use the "e" word—evangelism—without embarrassment. Shared suffering is *euangelion*, good news, *gospel*, in that it graces us with the capacity to experience and engage those outside and beyond as fellow strugglers. Shared suffering inspires us to slowly but surely befriend the world with increasingly compassionate hearts that grow progressively hungrier for justice for all. First at the back of the sanctuary of the world's pain, next as passersby, then as guarded company, finally as undefended presence.

Our evangelistic crusade—yes I said it—is an unarmed one. We do not use conventional missionary missiles—a targeted message and market-savvy method. Rather, we broaden the borders of relationship to encompass spaces in which we are willing to be more susceptible to strangers and strangers are able to be more defenseless among us.

Following Ronnie's discovery of the bond he shared with Johnny, the shield behind which Ronnie existed was carefully lowered to expose himself to more and more of Johnny's character. By remaining open to Ronnie's courageous, though cautious, advance, the wall around the space in which Johnny existed cracked here and there to let in more and more of Ronnie's life as it really was. Through their presence together in the common terrain that contained each of their vulnerabilities, vulnerabilities occasionally colliding but more often shared, the dawn of a hospice community's healing drew nearer. Ronnie and Johnny have given us a good map onto the mission field.

Every now and then, I follow it. Take, for instance, my walk down the street for a late morning coffee break. I put a quarter in homeless Frank's cup. We strike up a conversation about the Red Sox's off-season trades, and I discover—again—that the major difference between Frank and me is the four walls behind which I retreat at the end of the day.

As I head on down the street to Starbucks, I realize that our careless banter stretches the margins of my life to a circumference that encompasses more and more of the township of Frank's spirit. I imagine that Frank, after several more of our conversations over a long period of time, may trust my intentions enough to enlarge the perimeter of his life to encompass a greater dimension of my existence. One day the quarter I drop in his cup may seem a little more like help from a friend than a hand down from a "suit."

The friendship between Ronnie and Johnny is an icon that humanizes our prayerful intentions for the world. It is an image that moves us away from a sense of "oughtness" in response to the world's pain to a place of genuine engagement in the world's pain. Blest be the tie that binds and rebuilds a broken world.

4 ❧

God's Time and Our Times

So you have pain now, but I will see you again and your hearts will rejoice, and no one will take your joy from you.

John 16:22

"**I** asked my mom what she thought about me wearing this hat to Grandma's funeral, because it is a whole lot of hat."[1] And it is. The hat has a center mountain of woven satin with streams of the same material cascading across and over an undulating, leopard-patterned brim of velvet almost two feet in diameter.

As a rule, black women wear wonderful hats to church. They are mostly hardworking, working-class women, who, as Maya Angelou wrote, "work large and are paid small."[2] Sundays are their time to be adorned and adored. The hat is their Sunday crown:

---

1. Deirdre Guion, in *Crowns: Portraits of Black Women in Church Hats*, by Michael Cunningham and Craig Marberry (New York:Doubleday, 2000), 128.
2. Maya Angelou, from "Foreword," Ibid., 2.

After the bath, after rubbing down her arms, legs, and neck with sweet-smelling lotions; after she has put on her best underclothes (don't wear raggedy underclothes—you may be in an accident and have to go to the hospital, and what would the nurses and doctors think of you if you had safety pins in your brassiere?), she is ready. She dresses in the finest Sunday church clothes she owns, layers her face with Fashion Fair cosmetics and sprays herself with wonderful perfume, and then she puts on THE HAT, and it is The Hat.[3]

Black women and the hats they wear to church are expressive of an easily defended axiom: The more marginalized and oppressed the community is, the more jubilant are its ritual events and rights of passage, the more opulent and exuberant are the members in attendance.

I learned this truth in the Jim Crow South. In Albany, Georgia, on Wednesday evenings, when my mother and I would take "the maid" back to her shack on an either very dusty or muddy road in "colored town," we would pass the church house during "Prayer Meeting." From inside the worn out, white clapboard building came some of the richest harmony and most soulful singing imaginable.

I was fascinated by this truth in the poor South. During vacations to my father's family on the cotton mill village in eastern North Carolina, my brother and I would sometimes hide in the bushes beside the big tent, its flaps up, under which the traveling evangelist was holding "tent meeting." We would watch wide-eyed as the swirling, shouting, and swaying flock was "slain by the Spirit."

I celebrated this truth by attending a few Halloween Parties in the gay community during the early years of

---

3. Ibid.

the AIDS pandemic, when the disease was mostly confined to them. The costumes were more outlandish and
the atmosphere more flamboyant than ever.

I was inspired by this truth while barely inside the
large gymnasium in which thousands of participants in
the three-day breast cancer walk waited for the closing
ceremonies to begin. The spirit of the place was no less
lively than the Gator Bowl just before kick off at the an-
nual Georgia-Florida football game.

The more oppressed we are by the little and not so
little deaths and bereavements of everyday life, the more
we find cause to celebrate a contradicting reality here
and there. We, who experience the injustices of "earth"
that bend and break us, are quicker to commemorate,
now and then, the justice of "heaven" that "makes the
crooked straight." We, who are caught short by realities
beyond our design and control, desire to have held before
us the wholeness that divine love holds out for us. We,
whose best laid plans, whose put-together lives, whose
carefully considered and cultivated relations have been
stolen by existence, more willingly submit our times of
diminishment to a time set apart for divine love's extrava-
gance. The spirit we bring to Sabbath, when and as we
are conversant with our multifarious deaths and bereavements, is like that of black women in church hats.

The sanctuary where we wear our crowns sometimes
is more than architectural space. Sanctuary can be off to
the side of public events and passages. Sometimes sanctuary is conversation.

Joseph sat across from me in the prayer and meditation space at the far end of my study, a space set apart
from the meeting and counseling area by a sofa, and con-
taining objects and icons conducive to a worshipful environment. Joseph's commitment to Thomas had ended
after three years of struggle and hard work.

Our time together this particular afternoon was set aside to mark the end of Thomas and Joseph's relationship. For the occasion, Joseph brought his favorite picture, which is a scene from their commitment ceremony. Joseph, Thomas and I are standing at the altar. Thomas and Joseph have just shared vows. My priest's stole is wrapped around their joined hands as I pronounce them companions for life.

After sharing the picture and reminiscing about the ceremony and reception that followed, Joseph asked me if I thought what he had with Thomas was real. We silently sat with the question for several minutes. When we started talking about the question, we came to a mutual awareness that their relation was and still is real.

The fragile cup of Thomas and Joseph's different histories and particular wounds of spirit and psyche is not able to contain any longer the care they have for one another. Nonetheless, the genuineness of their love is held in the heart of God for eternity, as is the heaviness of the relation's failure. Over time, as God and Joseph attend to the ambiguity of the relation's beauty and brokenness, there is the promise that sadness will overcome despair, forgiveness will conquer blame, and fond story will reign over bad memory.

Our reverential contemplation of a picture that mirrored the wholeness of life and prayerful conversation about the brokenness of life offered Joseph more completion than finish to his relation with Thomas. Grief as something completed rather than finished can be returned to and touched—a gift. Grief as something finished is linear; something left behind and moved away from. Neglected grief reappears as a thud and reasserts as a sting.

Through a litany of conversation, Joseph rediscovered and hallowed *kairos* time, the fullness of time, conceded to and found consolation amidst *chronos* time, the march of time. Joseph fashioned an enigmatic crown of glory and suffering, roses and thorns, to wear on Sabbath. Joseph, by wearing such a crown, placed our times into the hands of God's time.

I honor Joseph's courage. I want to locate the nerve to adorn myself for Sabbath concerning relations I've left more finished than completed, relations that remain profaned, relations that I desire to consecrate again. In the valley of my relations are dry bones waiting for restoration in the reconciling heart of God. I imagine that you, too, have similar skeletal remains on the desert floor of your past relations.

Possibly now is the time for us go to the closet and pull out "THE HAT, and it is The Hat."

Good worship—whatever, wherever, and whoever the sanctuary—is the alliance of hope and grief celebrated by lame lives lurching and limping together towards Zion. When this liturgical balance is struck, we are wearing "a whole lot of hat," which, as James Baldwin reminds us, "has been bought and paid for."

5 &

Our Times

And about the ninth hour Jesus cried out with a loud
voice, "My God, my God, why have you forsaken me?"

Mark 15:34

Sometimes there are only thorns on the crown.

I remember the first clergy group in which I partici-
pated. I was an associate pastor in Savannah, Georgia. A
gathering composed of downtown clergy came together
once a month. One of us would present a paper, exegesis,
or idea that represented what was rising to the surface of
his (no women in the group) thoughts and prayers. I
chose to present a painting that hung off to the side of
my desk in the study, Picasso's *Guernica*.

I talked about the horror on the canvas, the senseless killing and destruction to which the canvas witnessed, and how Paul Tillich's interpretation of *Guernica*
sounded a strong tone in the temperament of my faith—
nevertheless. In spite of all the death and destruction humankind has visited in and upon history, Divine Love
does not give up on us. She still chooses to seek us out
with boundless desire and care. We have abandoned

God; nevertheless, God has not abandoned us.

There was a short silence after my presentation. Soon both rabbis in the group, one reformed and the other conservative, countered with their almost identical interpretations of the painting. They shared an element of Jewish spirituality, particularly prevalent since the Holocaust, which has to do with Yahweh having hit the road. God is so grossed out by humankind's endless evil that God has turned God's back in disgust. God has determined that God's creation of humankind has failed and is not worthy of any more effort to salvage it.

I noticed that the rabbis spoke of their spirituality of absence without an angst attached to it. God's gone-ness was a givenness that offered them and their congregations a means for praying the Holocausts of life for what they are, violent and virulent abysses void of even a pinch of hope, meaning, and resolution from heaven.

The spirituality of the rabbis served me well later on in my ministry, when I would spend years among those who died too painfully, young, alone, wasted, and maligned. The spirituality of the AIDS hospice was Gethsemane and Golgotha without the miracle of Easter morning a mere day's wait away. Sometimes the only Easter we got emerged from within the experiences of Gethsemane and Golgotha, not beyond them, emerged there as the durable peace of a shared sorrow that resisted and refused any softeners.

Gregory wondered if he would live long enough to celebrate his twenty-sixth birthday, three weeks away. His wish was that he would, even though he was very tired. His desire was that his parents would drive up from Savannah to celebrate with him. His fear was that if he asked them, they would not be able to come. They would find another excuse like the ones they usually gave since they found out, in the course of one brief conversation, that he was gay and HIV positive. After talking it through, he decided not to ask them, saying that he did not have room for another rejection before he died. A few of us shared cake and ice cream with Gregory several days later, in case he didn't make it to his birthday. Sometimes such peace was enough; sometimes it was not. We took what we could get.

I usually didn't share stories such as Gregory's outside the hospice community. When I did, those who heard them mostly wondered why I would want to do such morbid work. I remember being at the symphony with some of my best friends, Jim and Denise. During Hindemith's "When Lilacs Last in the Dooryard Bloom'd," based on Walt Whitman's poem, Denise whispered, "Only Bill appreciates this gloom and doom; I'm ready to go."

I know Denise's sentiment. It's mine. I, too, often try to dodge the darkness that is the spirituality of absence. Yet, I've learned that too much avoidance of the sediment of sadness underneath a surface engagement with existence doesn't serve anybody well for long.

Ours is a populace that fiercely strives to shake off solemnity. We relentlessly pursue happiness and contentment as a veneer over anxiety; anxiety being a stale and soured sadness. The truth of Flannery O'Connor's diagnosis of our culture, some fifty years ago, in the essay, "Novelist and Believer," grows in relevance and significance: "Ours...is an age that has domesticated despair and learned to live with it happily."[1]

Religion needs to stomp on the toes of us who are in such a frenzied race for facile fulfillment. Our faith communities do have a few sacred rites and rituals that sim-

---

1. Flannery O'Connor. *Mystery and Manners* (New York:The Noonday Press, 1970), 159.

ply honor (and no more) the solemnity that falls on any heart that honestly looks around. They are of inestimable value to a culture that has damned up despondency to disastrous results. Valuable because our friends and lovers, our guilds and gatherings, are not that good at hearing more than a modicum of our sighs. "Church" can bear the weight of a spirituality of absence. And church, being where two or three are gathered, also can happen here and there between her public liturgies. A few folks can recite and abide together the angst of living that is the soul of, say, Psalm 13.

Sometimes I wish I could isolate the Maundy Thursday rite of the stripping of the altar from the blessed assurance of that which is to come very shortly. So shortly that the lilies already are crowded into, and waiting in, the same sacristy to which we just brought the stripped paraments and appointments of victory.

The curtain in the temple is hardly ever torn long enough to turn our hearts.

6 ✏

Holding Out
for Connection

When Joseph woke from sleep, he did as the angel of the
Lord commanded him; he took his wife, but knew her not
until she had borne a son; and he called his name Jesus.

Matthew 1:24-25

I noticed at the hospice interdisciplinary meeting that
Tim, the medical director, was preoccupied. His contributions to the conversations about those we cared for
were less spirited than usual. He re-engaged when it
came time for the team to review our care of Michael.

Tim had just returned from a home visit with
Michael. Michael had asked Tim to help him take his life
when the symptoms of AIDS started to take a turn from
bad to worse. Michael recently had moved back to Atlanta after his lover, Samuel, died from AIDS in Los An-
geles. Michael said that he did not want to experience
what Samuel had gone through. When it came to the
point of wasting away to nothing, losing his sight, suffer-

ing with dementia, or needing to wear diapers, he wanted to take charge of his own death.

The team's response to Tim was fervent. Three positions emerged, each well reasoned, strongly defended, and earnestly debated. Some members of the team said that the situation was a no brainer. Simply follow the protocol, which stated that any mention of suicide must be reported and followed up by the psychiatric service.

Others felt that Michael's request was an opportunity for Tim to establish a deeper connection with Michael. By engaging Michael about what he experienced Samuel's death to be like, what he imagined his own death would be like, what he feared the most, how he wanted to manage the coming days including or not including suicide, Michael would be in a better place, a clearer and wiser position, to decide about his future.

The rest felt that Tim should help Michael kill himself. Not in a Kevorkian manner, but through Tim's simple acknowledgment that storage of some of the medications Michael now took amounted to enough to over dose when he desired.

As the leader of the team, I could take one of three positions. Impose the organization's suicide policy and be done with it. Put on my mediating hat and lead the team towards a decision that might not be unanimously supported but at least arrived at mutually. Grow my leadership arms long and strong enough to hold the team dynamic through and beyond the meeting, trusting that insight would emerge through ongoing engagement.

I chose the latter, leaning hard into philosopher Hannah Arendt's definition of truth: "Truth is one person speaking, another listening and speaking in turn." After many episodes similar to Michael and the hospice team, I found it both easier and essential to practice what Hannah Arendt preached.

Stewards of the community of the dying and bereaved are required to create and sustain a relational space that is ample enough to hold what is, whatever it is. The same is required for the stewardship of all environments composed of compromised people. Compromised people make up all the environments of which I've been a part.

When those among us are broken or bewildered, and come to us for consolation, our strongest desire—their healing and wholeness—fuels our resolve to curb or cure whatever crisis they are in. And, most of us know through experience, what it is like to see the needy eyes of diminished ones glaze over when we get busy with their problems. Connection can be quickly lost through decisive, outcome-oriented care.

The fragments of a person or community's fractured spirit coalesce in a setting that simply contains sorrow, uncertainty and suffering. The seeds of healing germinate as healers merely hold a constant and predictable environment for those who hurt. So much presence requires so little action. So little action requires tremendous strength. The staying power of presence must withstand the barrages of conscience, good sense, and convention that come both from within the healers and their wider social network.

Joseph, the husband of Mary, the father of Jesus, is a patron saint for those who strive to hold out for no more or less than relation with and for those who seek their company in troubling times. Joseph's wife comes home with news of her pregnancy by God. Initially determined to do away with Mary through divorce, his testicular right and privilege, Joseph wakes from a nap willing to stand with her on ground outside the precepts of their clan. When called to a truth too startling and stark to be secured by tradition, Joseph looked backwards and forwards, took deep breaths, and stood still at her side.

Recently, I visited the studio of a sculptor in New Hampshire, whose medium is wood. She had carved from an old tree trunk a big and bulky Joseph tenderly holding the infant Jesus. Joseph looked down at his child in awe. Jesus looked up with wide-eyed curiosity.

I wonder how many similar scenes of wonder we have denied ourselves and others by stands for truth, determinations towards resolve, ejaculations of righteousness that preclude and preempt relation with compromised people who come to us for...relation. I think of encounters I would like the chance to redeem, presumptions of care that have cut off relation with those I love, and with those whose well being was to be sheltered on my watch.

I'm mindful of a daughter whom I believed needed to know more facts than she did. I remember more than one fit of determination to resolve parish conflicts or mediate parishioners' quarrels that needed more space for and time in dialogue than resolution could give. I'm ashamed that I've stood my ground with lovers, friends, family and congregants because of conviction.

I have gained some wisdom by suffering through the sins of willfulness. Clarity, understanding, intimacy—legitimate needs and realistic expectations—are less important than, and sometimes worth forfeiting for, connection. What really needs to be said or done usually is an indicator that it would be better left unsaid and undone, if relation is the desired outcome. The meaning, reason, purpose and desire that each person or party brings to relation deserve to be explored and respected by the other or others, instead of or before they need to be negotiated.

The wisdom seems to work regardless of the context. What enables a parent and child, mates, or members of a community to stay in relation probably is not an altogether ineffective paradigm for advancing unlikely alliances like Trent Lott and Ted Kennedy, Bishop Spong and Pat Robinson, *Shrub* (George W. Bush) and Saddam, Israel and Palestine.

The hospice team, over time, talked ourselves into a presence with Michael that would have been precluded by assent to either the truths of program protocol or progressive, right to die practice. Michael died a good death by means of a circle of companions, who held out for connection and held themselves together through connection.

7 ✺

Boundaries and
Being Loved

*This is my commandment, that you love one another as
I have loved you.*
                         . John 15:12

While on sabbatical last year, I occasionally took
friendly walks on the beach with the senior church warden, with the mutually-established condition that we
would not talk about church matters. In today's boundary-obsessed church, due to the high incident of clergy
sexual abuse and misconduct, such a walk is considered
a "boundary lapse."

The logic goes like this. The pastor can offer care to
parishioners. Boundaries are crossed when pastor and
parishioner care for one another. An environment of mutuality is dangerous.

Carter Heyward, in her controversial book, *When
Boundaries Betray Us*, argues that the model of the dis-
tanced, well-bounded healer, who gives but dares not re-

ceive care, is at its heart abusive. The arrangement precludes the person seeking care from being fully human—loving!—in the immediacy of the healing encounter. I agree.

The model of the distant healer, the giver but not receiver of care, made its way into the literature and training of pastoral leaders long before the era of openness and honesty about the problem of clergy sexual misconduct with congregants. Some would argue that the normative position of parent-like pastors with disproportionate power over parishioners set the stage for the abuse that came into greater light in the last ten to fifteen years.

A dominant cliché during my days in seminary was, "Don't take your shoes off with parishioners." The practical reason was that friendships with some parishioners would make other parishioners jealous. Reasonable enough. The theoretical underpinning of the cliché suggests that too much closeness between pastor and parishioners results in the loss of the objectivity and distance needed to direct and prosper a parish's life. If such a definition of leadership looks like that practiced by Ward Cleaver in television's 50s and 60s sitcom, "Leave it to Beaver," that's because it is. Pastors disdain the projections upon us of father-on-a-pedestal, yet we continue to present ourselves as an icon of the same.

Dying and bereaved people have a bone to pick with those who advise or defend care that is less than mutual. They have little patience with healers who use a managed, one-dimensional, dissonant "presence" with them as that which, like a magnet to metal filings, coalesces the fragmented and fragile elements of their "selves" into a unified whole better capable of a maintaining a sufficient life. For dying and bereaved people, who live in the land of shared insufficiency, wholeness (salvation!) is experienced now as interdependent, co-creating persons.

Wholeness, as something sought after by the achievement of a more cohesive, individuated self through submission to one who values and practices the giving but not receiving of unconditional positive regard has little appeal and less value.

Boundaries that limit care to the pastor, which create a parental, dominant dynamic, might well be more lightly drawn so that the pastor cares and is cared for in relation rather than accolade. This allows the full humanity of the pastor and parishioners to participate in the liberating encounter of mutual relation.

My experience with Martin represents lines more lightly drawn. Martin came to me for grief counseling after the death of his lover to AIDS. Over time, the parameters of the helping relationship softened. Martin became less a counselee and more a friend.

My most meaningful experience with Martin was near the time of his own death from AIDS. I picked up Martin from the AIDS clinic, where he had gone for a treatment to counteract his increasing loss of vision. Martin insisted on taking me to lunch. For two hours he coached my soul from the bench of his dying, a soul that had become wearied in a health-care position that was mostly about administration and marketing. The care and courage he gave me that day became a foundation on which I built the decision to return to full-time pastoral ministry.

Martin's dying did not "excuse" our crossing of traditional boundaries. Rather, his dying poured us into a crucible of caring that transcends and makes moot many of the established boundaries of pastor and parish relating. I believe this crucible is the right container not only for care of the dying but for pastors who participate as one among many parishioners who experience the deaths and losses of daily life.

And what about the issue of clergy friendships with

some parishioners creating jealousy among others? As a parent of three children, I am aware of how much attention I am paying to each, and, at times, I'm aware that they are paying the same attention to me. Sibling rivalry is a reality. As an adult friend, I'm not aware that I do much monitoring of how much attention I am paying to each of my friends so as not to pay more attention to some than others. Nor, am I aware that they are concerned with how much attention I am paying to whom.

Pastors who are put or put themselves into the role of objective, distant, unavailable parent-figure are accurately perceived as crossing boundaries when they spend more time with some congregants than others. Pastors who either assent to or create inhuman boundaries are sure to cross them through "lapses of humanity" that, in other communities or organizations, are considered merely convivial. We unnecessarily make malignant what is normally benign. Furthermore, the dominant, parent-like position of the pastor creates the dynamic of rivalry between infantilized parishioners. Such pastoral posture, I'm convinced, has something to do with otherwise exceedingly mature people regressing to childlike behavior in parish settings.

When pastors refuse to accept the mantle of "Herr Pastor" or work to deconstruct it, the foundation upon which the boundary between pastor and parishioner is built erodes. Pastors who are parish participants in the interdependent dynamic of shared insufficiency are on their way towards congregational relating that is not tainted with boundary policy and policing. These pastors are left to ask themselves what constitutes respectful and realistic relations with parishioners, and how are they are to be good stewards of the inherent power of their position in these relations.

Pastors do well by others and for self when we deflect the deference that comes our way because of a position held. A deflected deference precludes the power to harm that comes with another's more or less blind regard for our station in the church.

Lay persons do well to relate to us in a manner that is no different from how they might communicate with their neighbor, colleague, or one with whom they covenant for particular services rendered, expecting no more or less from us than they would expect of them. Through a great lessening of the immense mother/father baggage transferred upon us, parishioners are better able to secure a safe, confidential space in which they can draw upon our experience and expertise as a healing presence in times of transition and trouble.

Pastors and parishioners in mutual relations make for a more delicate dance, particularly in the present boundary-obsessed environment. The one-way street of *agape* seems safer than the two way street that is *eros*. In South Georgia, the saying goes, "Where there are the meanest rattlesnakes there also are the best blackberries." The wisdom therein is not to avoid the patch, but to be very cautious in picking.

8 ❧

Spilling or Sharing

Carry no purse, no bag, no sandals; and greet no one on the road. Whatever house you enter, first say, "Peace be to this house!"   Luke 10:4-6

I had been on board at a psychiatric hospital for only a week and was trying my hardest to make connections with patients, clinicians, and colleagues. I figured that a great way to establish myself was through the sermon I was to preach on Sunday morning.

The sermon mostly was about my own emotional struggles. I felt that by offering up my own woundedness, I would establish a bond with both the patients and those who cared for them. I noticed, as I was delivering the sermon, that some in attendance became uncomfortable, others seemed to tune out, a few left the room.

A couple of days later, my supervisor said that I should "be careful not to drop my pants in the pulpit out of my need to find community in a new and scary place." He said that too many of the patients had been hurt by family, friends, and healers who had used them as vessels into which pour their unmanaged needs.

I have since learned to ask myself some basic questions. Who is benefiting from my transparency, self or relation? Do I control my brokenness or does it control me? Does the sharing of my insufficiency create enmeshment or mutuality? Am I far enough away from the story of my woundedness to keep a critical eye on what's going on in the relation? Does my shared suffering bog down the relation in sympathetic banter or move it to holier ground?

As careful as we are, there are times when the answers to these questions are ones we don't want to hear. Relations with certain people or environments tap needs too expansive for us to handle. At such times we are spilling rather than sharing.

In order to manage the spills, we are wise to have a "jury" to which we bring our relations for review. We empower the jury to critique our life in relation. My jury consists of people I've read, colleagues I trust, friends I depend on, my therapist, and my spiritual director.

People who participate in an interdependent web of shared insufficiency exist in an extraordinarily sensitive field of experience, which is dangerous to walk through in isolation. In fact, isolation is a good indicator of danger.

Healthy participation in the interdependent web of shared insufficiency is easier to point out than define. A good example is my present associate, Suzanne. I remember her first real engagement with the congregation we serve together. She was invited to the adult forum to share the spiritual path that led her to Emmanuel.

Suzanne shared a history of immense loss and struggle that had drawn her beyond the region of her own sufficiency and back into the community of a local congregation from which her journey towards ordination began. Yet her story was textured rather than laden, seasoned but not stale, convivial instead of off-putting, a confession, not an exposé. She was master of her own material in a way that invited relation. I know that Suzanne regularly submits her life in relation to confessor-friends.

Suzanne was invited to share her story of insufficiency. Mutual relation that moves to the deeper material of shared insufficiency is by invitation only. I like the way a hospice colleague, a director of volunteers, conveyed this imperative. Betsy gave new volunteers an image to hold on to in their relations with dying persons and their loved ones.

The image is of a guest walking to the door of a strange home to meet people who are experiencing the upheaval of one among them dying. The guest carries a suitcase of the self, which contains needs, desires, curiosities, expectations, and perceptions related to the people she or he will soon meet. After ringing the doorbell, the guest places the suitcase on the doorstep and walks into the home. By leaving the suitcase of self just outside the door, the guest can retrieve elements of his or her self as they are invited or summoned in to the relation.

Following Betsy's analogy, my sermon at the psychiatric hospital was akin to barging through the front door, suitcase in hand, and unpacking in the middle of the living room. I was not a good guest.

I learned a lot from my experience as the guest from hell. Since then, I remind myself, again and again, to try my best to cross the thresholds of my wounded neighbors' lives with arms bearing no more or less than respectful attention.

When I am able to bear no more or less than this, my presence gently whispers the scriptural salutation in a way that vulnerable ears can hear: "Peace be to this house!" When I am invited to share this peace beyond the doorstep, around the table of shared suffering, there are moments when it passes understanding.

9 ❧

The Agency of
Holy Anger

In the Temple he found those who were selling oxen
and sheep and pigeons, and the money-changers at
their business. And making a whip of cords, he drove
them all, with the sheep and oxen, out of the temple;
and he poured out the coins of the money-changers and
overturned their tables.
                                                    John 2:14-16

Paul approached me in great pain and small panic as I
made my way from one treatment room to the next in the
Friday morning AIDS clinic. He had a nasty case of the
thrush, a condition in which the gums become inflamed
and the mouth is one big toothache.

Paul wanted me to advocate for him at the reception
desk. His scheduled appointment was the following Friday. He was relying on his status as a counselee of mine
to make a way for him to be seen by a doctor or nurse
practitioner. I asked Paul why he warranted preferential

treatment. He threw his head back and opened his mouth wide like a little boy showing a sore throat to his mother. I looked around. The waiting room was jammed with scheduled patients. Most of them had troubles at least as serious as Paul's. The line for "drop-ins" was already out the door.

I told Paul that I didn't see that I could do anything that would aid his cause. I suggested that he might make a dent in the system by taking matters into his own hands. Half serious, half not, I mentioned that he could throw a fit in the middle of the floor, calling everybody from the governor to the clinic director a you-know-what for not providing enough space, time, and personnel to met the needs of AIDS patients. I advised him to make sure he included the hospital's CEO in the tirade. Paul went to work. His invectives made even the most seasoned among us blush and cringe. A doctor saw him in less than five minutes.

Paul's harangue has been the most effective paradigm for taking action and getting results for persons with HIV and AIDS. Jennifer, at 2:00 A.M., on the infectious disease floor of the county hospital, after asking for more pain medication three times and hearing each time that the medications were on the way, finally sent a water glass into the wall to adjust the protocol. Members of ACT UP, the AIDS activist group renowned for their radical actions, have carpeted the State Capitol's steps with bleach and hypodermic needles to encourage a breakthrough in the Senate's yearlong discussion of the morality of needle exchange.

In the AIDS community, I honed a spirituality of anger. I learned holy anger. Holy anger has a hold on the helplessness from which one's fury emanates. Holy anger moves out of helplessness to soften the edges and strengthen the resolve of irate hearts.

First, holy anger tempers. At the frayed end of another emerging outburst with a parishioner who has harassed me one too many times, I find the longest fiber of my rage, closely examine it, and discover a thread of impotence. I confess that I have no capacity to make anything good of the situation or relation. Once again, I am about to be swept away in a wash of emotions. Praying the impotence enables me to focus on myself more than the antagonist. I endure, again, the situation and person who has rankled my feathers. Again, I am kept from compromising my leadership of the parish. Later, I share my impotence with a colleague, who is stuck in a back and forth banter with a board member. We establish an empathic bond that we can draw upon in the future when our goats are about to be gotten.

In the aftermath of a scrap with my mate, I trace my affect—greater than the present encounter justifies—back to times in my childhood when I felt isolated, unheard, looked over and past in a home that had many broken places. Praying the pain of that afraid and lonely child enables an ashamed adult to make amends. By continuing to pray for my wounded child within, I narrow the gap between experience and affect that is opened in certain situations.

Second, holy anger solidifies one's ability to advocate for weak and diminished people. The afternoons I spent threatening insurance companies with every kind of public disclosure when they initially refused to cover new medications that would greatly improve the quality of AIDS patients' lives prepared me to acquire adequate nursing care when my father-in-law returned from the hospital. I would not take no for an answer when the director of the home health agency said that they do not visit on days patients return from the hospital, because Medicare does not reimburse for those visits.

The holy anger that issues from the AIDS community invites and equips us to hallow our anger. Sandra
was dying from AIDS contracted from her husband, who
was infected by using dirty needles. Sandra's hot tears
burned the chest of the home health aid, who held her
close while she confessed complete assurance that her
once again "high" husband would never be able to care
for their four children after she died. Our mindfulness of
Sandra may help us find and hold onto the helplessness
at the heart of our anger.

Robert had just died from AIDS. The medical director of the hospice and Robert's father stood over his bed.
The father demanded that the medical director not put
AIDS as the cause of death on the death certificate.
Robert's mother was afraid that the "truth" might get
back to their retirement community in Florida, compromising their comfort there. The medical director, knowing how hard Robert had worked to gain acceptance for
himself and others, typed "AIDS" in capital letters on the
certificate, and mailed a copy to the home of his parents.
Our mindfulness of the medical director may help us
find the courage to unleash our anger to advance the
causes of the disenfranchised ones.

There is good news for Paul, Jennifer, ACT UP, Sandra, Robert, the medical director, and all of us each time
our anger leads us to prayers of personal helplessness and
public action for the powerless ones. We have an advocate
in, under, around, and through us—the disturbed and disturbing Spirit of an enraged and outrageous Jesus.

10 &

Praying Powerlessness

Going a little farther Jesus fell on his face and prayed,
"My Father, if it is possible, let this cup pass from me;
nevertheless, not as I will, but as thou wilt."

Matthew 26:39

I was sitting with a fellow pastor in spiritual direction.
He was sharing the content and aftermath of his Thanksgiving sermon. He was unsettled by the disclosure of his
orphaned childhood, which, he said, left him "hanging
out there," exposed. More unsettling was the emotional
turmoil caused by the memories that resurfaced following the sermon. He said that his therapist equated the re-
actions to post-traumatic stress syndrome. As he was
sharing the experience with me, his hands were cupped
in the shape of a chalice and raised about three inches
from his lap.

After sharing the experience of the Thanksgiving sermon, he started to communicate a concern about his
prayer life. He wanted to develop a more regular discipline of praying some aspects of the daily office, like
noonday prayer and compline. As he talked, his hands re-

mained in the chalice-like position.

We talked about the juxtaposition of his hands and the desire for a more rote and regimented prayer practice. We acknowledged our mutual experience of unconsciously fleeing from prayerfulness that emanates from the dark regions of our helplessness. We shared how painful it is to prayerfully drink from the chalice of his hands. We affirmed that the chalice, as heavy as it is to hold, can be a "cup of salvation," a drink by which the enlightenment and accompaniment of grace sometimes quenches our thirst.

How proficient I am at praying around my powerlessness. A well-defended place in me goes around rather than through the thicket to reach the fulfillment held out by prayer's promise. After decades of being shortchanged by such avoidance, I still think I can beat the odds.

The tenacity of my gamble is in proportion to the sweaty road that is prayer as the via negativa, the way of negation. The via negativa is the journey beyond the light of our control, the path into the dark, untamed regions of our unknowing and unsettledness, the route into God's clouded, unknowable, and unsettling character. Who wants to go there? One is reminded of the place where the Gospel of Mark originally ended, 16:8, at the empty tomb, whereupon they were afraid. No wonder others came along to cover such nakedness with the nice clothes of twenty-one reassuring, fulfilling verses of resolution.

Persons who are dying become the chalice-like hands of my friend. Their lives are a prayer of powerlessness. Nonetheless, the prayer is one of peace. Belden Lane writes:

> It is a deep mystery that love is born in the mind's (and body's) experience of emptiness and loss. The longing of the soul, made sharper by the painful absence of that which it loves—by its inability to close

on what it desires—reaches in darkness for a beloved who comes unannounced and without guarantee. God reaches through the dark night of the senses, as John of the Cross would express it, to offer freely in love what no human effort could buy. If God is to be loved as God loves, it will happen only in the dark corridors of emptiness. Only in devastating loss—beyond all security of language and identity, in despairing ever of obtaining the glory first sought—only then does a truth too wondrous to be grasped come rushing back out of the void. Love takes wing where calculation ends.[1]

How firmly dying persons initially hold onto their mind, body, and relations as they have known them. When these treasures inevitably slip beyond their firmest grip, defiance and despair gradually are drowned out by an emerging acquiescence. Their vulnerable and exposed hearts come to exude a lightness of being. Their hearts express a widening smile and curiosity that embrace approaching death like an eight-year-old waiting for the circus to begin. T.S. Eliot, writing in *East Coker*: "In my end is my beginning."

Dying persons teach us, with their lives, to pray in a region beyond our control, on the other side of language and understanding.

Forsaking language in prayer is an opening to the impotence that liberates. Sam Keen writes:

> A psychoanalysis of chatter would suggest that our over-verbalization is an effort to avoid something which is fearful—silence. But why should silence be threatening? Because words are a way of structuring, manipulating, and controlling; thus, when they are absent the specter of loss of control arises. If we can-

---

1. Belden Lane. *The Solace of Fierce Landscapes* (Oxford University Press: Oxford and New York, 1998), 73.

not name it, we cannot control it. Naming gives us power. Hence, silence is impotence, the surrender of control. Control is power, and power is safety.[2]

Sometimes I come to prayer to untie my tongue about matters of the heart, so that I can say and God can hear what's going on. Other times I remember to put a figurative pebble in my mouth before prayer, that I might stammer my way to a baffling silence into which God might speak.

Beginning prayer where our understanding of God ends is an opening to the powerlessness that redeems. Saint Augustine wrote, "If you have understood, then this is not God. If you were able to understand, then you understood something else instead of God. If you were able to understand even partially, then you have deceived yourself with your own thoughts."[3]

In prayer, I usually grapple to grasp awareness and discern direction. Why am I so sad? What must I do? I am less likely to enter prayer on the heels of Saint Bonaventure's wisdom: *Ego dormio, sed cor meum vigilat* — As the ego sleeps, the heart remains vigilant.[4]

Prayer that begins in the stillness beyond language and understanding is a gift to the world, because it has a propensity to end in resolute action. Life prayed in the territory beyond ego exhibits a freedom dangerous to the "powers and principalities" that depend on selves who are concerned about image, sufficiency, identity, and stability. Thomas Merton said that such a desert is "a base for observation of a corrupt society."[5]

---

2. Sam Keen, *To A Dancing God* (New York: Harper & Row, 1970), 44. Cited in Lane, 68-69.

3. Lane, 68.

4. Ibid., 72.

5. Raymond Bailey, *Thomas Merton on Mysticism* (Garden City, NY: Doubleday, 1975), 54. Cited in Lane, 77.

Life prayed in the desert beyond ego has the truest impulse toward compassion and justice, because there is nothing to register the consequences to self that come with taking on the demons downstairs, next door, at city hall, or in the impenetrable bureaucracies and gigantic corporations that are wired to dominate and influence. The stuttering sounds and babbling noise of those who have encountered grace just over the margins of their proficiency grate on the nerve centers of oppressive systems. Those at the controls of these systems expect and assume that ego-invested souls will, at worst, put up with them as a necessary evil.

At my parish, we often think of our extensive and, by my estimation, amazing music program to be one of our principle outreach programs. We believe, as the poet Mary Oliver has written, that music moves towards silence. Music transports us to an ecstatic stillness beyond our ego-invested selves from which we discover greater liberty to move back into the ordinary world as more reckless prophets of and for the Good.

Resist prayer that is weighted too much towards power and glory. Such prayer doesn't allow us to drink enough from the chalice of our powerlessness, crafted from silver mined from the deepest veins of our lived experience, holding the nectar of heaven. We don't want something so precious to tarnish in the cabinet of an ostensibly happy life.

11 ↷

Re-enchanting Persons

No one puts new wine into old wineskins. Otherwise,
the wine will burst the skins, and the wine is lost, and
so are the skins; but one puts new wine into fresh skins.

Mark 2:22

I was in the elevator on my way up to visit a parishioner who was dying of an insidious staph infection that was prevailing against the strongest antibiotics. She caught the infection from a routine breast biopsy. Most likely, the needle used in the procedure was not properly sterilized.

When the elevator stopped at my floor, the door opened to a group of medical residents. From their midst I heard one say, "Did you see the sepsis in bed 642?" The "sepsis in bed 642" was my dear friend who was dying. A funny, intelligent, complex, sometimes depressed, deeply sensitive, occasionally cantankerous, compassionate, wonderfully engaging wife, mother, daughter, friend, architect, hospice volunteer, and artist had been reduced to a diagnosis. I saw red.

I have witnessed so many dying persons suffer from the reductionist relationship caregivers take to them through their illness. Caregivers are likely to give undue attention to the accidents of one's ailment rather than the essence of one's being. The social worker's initial assessment of Charles was variations on the theme of "addicted and prone to violence." I tiptoed around Charles for seven months. Undue attention to incidental matters, however fundamental and striking they may seem, can cause the dying person's soul to waste away from neglect. I have watched some folks die spiritual deaths before biological ones.

Of course, diagnosis is not ill intended. It is one way healers get a small handle on and some meager control over the staggering amount of immense human suffering and impossible-to-understand-and-integrate experience encountered in the course of a day. If you name an overwhelming encounter, you're a bit closer to dominating it. Why else would Yahweh be so rude to Moses at the burning bush, when Moses innocently asked God's name?

Healers do not have the franchise on diagnosis. When we confront difficult and complex people, we seek to pinpoint their peccadilloes and peculiarities in order to persevere and protect ourselves. We use various dimensions of diagnosis to demystify the more muddled, unpredictable, and indefinable phenomena of their presence, which has us either flummoxed or fuming. From such a perch, we approach and engage them towards predetermined ends. By freezing the frame of reference, we limit the possibilities of encounter and connection. We make it harder for the Spirit to enrich and renew our relations with people who trigger parts of us that may need attention, care, and healing.

When I've been disappointed, hurt, or discombobulated by someone, I am quick to go to work on her or his psyche, upbringing, issues, habits, and motivations. All the better when there is a confidant near to hear my description of, and remedy for, the one I am vilifying. My father's abusiveness? He's narcissistic. A parishioner's incessant criticism? Entitled by class.

Prayerful scrutiny of my fits of diagnostic zeal cracks open the window of my defended spirit, allowing a little fresh air to blow through the room of my stolid and stormy relations. Such analytic prayer is not as busy as it seems. It is simply sitting still in the stuffiness of interpersonal dilemma. God's silence meets mine and there is a brief whiff of the lilacs outside. Let's see, could my father's abusiveness when I was young fuel my automatic reaction to the parishioner's criticisms? And might that bruised little boy within benefit from a little attention from the man in whom he resides?

When I risk letting those who injure and disturb me mirror my own woundedness, they become no more or less mysterious than me. The novelist Walker Percy wrote that we know more about black holes in space than ourselves. If there is even a hint of truth to Percy's diagnosis, it is presumptuous to think I can whisper one categorical thing about myself, much less my neighbor.

The mystery of humankind invites us to encounter, albeit cautiously, the other as, well, the other, the *mysterium tremendum et fascinans*. By accepting the invitation, we enchant the sister or brother with whom we are in relation. We re-enchant the sister or brother we have slotted in order to subdue. When the other remains the other, she or he is freed from an inordinate power to curse us and occasionally is liberated to bless us.

I'm remembering Bill and Raymond. Bill was the senior pastor at the first parish I served after seminary, as associate pastor. Even though Bill was never anything but kind and fair to me, I hardly ever related to him outside the box in which I placed him, overweight and controlling; two adjectives I often fear might be assigned to

me if I'm not diligent. I don't think we would have ever
been good friends. Nonetheless, I deeply regret the pain
I caused him by paralyzing our partnership with the dart
of my diagnosis. Bill died a young death to colon cancer.
He died knowing me as little more than an overly judg-
mental associate.

Raymond lived in the housing projects of Atlanta. He
was black, poor, uneducated, and full of cancer. I was his
hospice volunteer. He could have easily and understand-
ably sized me up as white, well-off, educated, and
healthy, and could have initially related to me on those
terms. Instead, Raymond was wise enough to be respect-
fully curious of my presence in his home. He granted us
the freedom to forge a connection uncontaminated by a
predetermination of who I was. His attention to the
essence of my presence rather than the accidents of my
life helped me to do the same. We became fast friends.

In the sacrament of baptism, we covenant to respect
the dignity of every human being. This aspect of our bap-
tismal vows summons us beyond our assurances about
and estimations of neighbor onto the mysterious ground
of their being. There we are encouraged to take off our
shoes, sometimes anxiously, other times expectantly, and
wait for the Spirit to blow when and where She pleases.
When She does, we rarely need to reach for a jacket.

12 ❧

Caring and Not Caring

*The Pharisees and scribes said to Jesus, "The disciples
of John fast often and offer prayers, and so do the disciples of the Pharisees, but yours eat and drink."*

Luke 5:33

In these days of corporate corruption the movie *Bul-worth* is a fitting tale. The story is about U.S. Senator Jay Bulworth, who is running for re-election. He is de-pressed; so depressed that he takes out a huge insurance policy on himself, with his daughter as beneficiary, and hires a hit man to do him in.

During the days that follow, Bulworth realizes that pending death precludes the need to be politic on the campaign trail. He starts to tell the truth, finds great de-light in talking about the way things are. He says that the voter really doesn't have a say in the process. The country is being run by special interest groups with the most money to give to the candidates' coffers—two in particu-lar, the insurance and pharmaceutical industries.

Bulworth rediscovers his liberal roots in earnest and

with a courage and conviction about them that had previously escaped him. Now he wants to live, really live. In the end, while trying to cancel the contract on his head, he is killed by a lobbyist for the insurance industry who is incensed that Bulworth now ignores him.

Pending death answered for Bulworth the extraordinary prayer of T.S. Eliot, in his poem, *Ash Wednesday*: "Teach me to care and not to care."

The community of the dying and bereaved helps answer T.S. Eliot's prayer for us who suffer the consequences of our own skewed concerns, we who more or less tolerate the twisted priorities of our nests and nation. Uprooted to the "fertile" desert of shared insufficiency, dying and bereaved persons flourish by learning to care for certain things and not for others. They develop the spiritual disciplines of the fourth-century desert mothers and fathers, *agrupnia* and *apatheia*, translated as divine attention and indifference by Belden Lane, in his book, *The Solace of Fierce Landscapes*. Through holy attention and indifference, they attain an integrity of relations that violates and transcends the recognized principles of the dominant culture.

As a pastor in the AIDS community, I witnessed, learned, and eventually practiced *agrupnia* and *apatheia*. I became indifferent to some of the religious norms of the dominant culture, and paid attention to various rituals of a marginalized society. I handed out brightly colored condoms, clean needles, and bleach as treats for the people I visited and counseled. I honored a colleague's decision to end his life when AIDS had robbed him of all he considered meaningful, and promised a severely painful death.

Among the dying and bereaved, I experienced what Kierkegaard, in his consideration of the Abraham and Isaac story of Genesis 22 in *Fear and Trembling*, called the "teleological suspension of the ethical." One detects a holy commandment in a particular situation that usurps universal mandates generally prescribed for God's people.[1] I held in abeyance the ethical imperatives of the Judeo-Christian tradition regarding sex, drugs and suicide for what I believed was the higher purpose of making well, being compassionate, doing justice.

Those who choose the Christian paradigm as a pattern for living find explicit precedent for the suspension of the ethical, especially in situations where church and society hinder the healing or wholeness of suffering people. Brother Jesus stood with and for broken people in ways that transcended and, as a result, transgressed the codes of religious purity and ritual cleanliness.

Jesus wrote the book on *apatheia* and *agrupnia*, flouting indifference towards, and paying attention to matters other than those prescribed by, sacred convention. Jesus, as we say in the South, went from "preaching to meddling" in regard to holy indifference and attention, and was executed. The controllers of sacred convention will tolerate heresy and immorality much more than they will endure disregard.

The integrity of our relations with and for suffering people, as well as our personal integrity as suffering persons, infers a radicalization of our devotion to Jesus as renegade. And, by that, I don't mean we find in Jesus free rein to ride into town and temple slinging our six shooters. Our radical devotion is more to Jesus than to rebellion. There is a difference.

The character of Jesus' apostasy was more understated and less manifest than we might think. Jesus chose to do what "Abba," his "Father in heaven," would have him do or not do in this or that situation. And, when confronted by authority for what he did or did not do, he

---

1. Louis Mackey, "The View from Pisgah" in *Kierkegaard: A Collection of Critical Essays*, edited by Josiah Thompson (Garden City, New York:Anchor Books, 1972), 412-413.

would not compromise. He kept doing and not doing.

Jesus' more crafty and anticlimactic revolution was not only purposeful; it was also politic. Authority is put in a pickle by honorable actions that turn over the applecart of convention. In reading the Gospels, one gets a sense that Jesus intrigued the authorities as much as he infuriated them. Even his execution seemed less like a judgment on his action, and more a prudent decision of those whose power was undermined.

The Christian's practice of *apatheia* and *agrupnia* is not directly confrontational. The discipline grows slowly in the soil of connection and blossoms as the flower of conviction.

As a priest, I preside at the blessings of same sex partners. In so doing, I am not tagging onto the liberal bandwagon. Nor am I racing down to diocesan headquarters to nail my cause to the cathedral doors. Rather, I'm doing what comes naturally after spending many years warming in the sun of gay relation.

My parish invites all persons to Eucharist. We are an open church not because we are driven to be on the leading edge of the church of the twenty-first century. Instead, our liturgy attracts many spiritually hungry people who are neither baptized nor Christian. It would be rude not to invite them to dinner.

The Christian practice of *apatheia* and *agrupnia* is not an agenda for justice and compassion. Instead, holy indifference and attention are by-products of life on the plentiful path to the place of the skull, practical actions of the pilgrim, which are subtly prophetic. They are indirectly disturbing in that they are grounded less in opinion and preachments and more in movement and action. In response to *apatheia* and *agrupnia*, people tend to push, pull, or get out of the way.

"Teach us to care and not to care."

13 ❧

The Profundity of Play

Martha was distracted with much serving; and she went to him and said, "Lord, do you not care that my sister has left me to serve alone? Tell her then to help me." But the Lord answered her, "Martha, Martha, you are anxious and troubled about many things; one thing is needful. Mary has chosen the good portion, which shall not be taken away from her."
                                                        Luke 10:40-42

Priscilla was a long-time, devoted member of my parish. I visited Priscilla in the nursing home for several years before her death. I noticed, several months before she died, that my place in her life was shared more and more with Wishbone.

Wishbone was Priscilla's stuffed animal; not just any stuffed animal—a Jack Russell terrier with an FAO Schwartz pedigree. Priscilla adored Wishbone. Whenever I would go to see Priscilla during the months before her death, Priscilla and Wishbone hosted me. Priscilla would be cradling Wishbone, stroking Wishbone while she listened to me and occasionally spoke. After awhile, as I got more comfortable with Wishbone, I, too, would reach over and pat him while conversing with Priscilla. I learned that the best way to arouse Priscilla's spirits, the easiest way to spark conversation, was to ask about how Wishbone was doing.

Some parishioners returned from visiting Priscilla fearing that she had regressed back to her childhood. I tried to dull, or at least deflect, their more logical interpretation of Priscilla and Wishbone's delightful dance of spirits. I expressed my desire to head for the toy store myself, but for a basset hound instead. I suggested that Priscilla was reveling in the holy region in all of us where our child within waits to dance us through the dark forests of life.

Psychoanalyst Donald Winnicott had important and encouraging things to say about what went on between Priscilla and Wishbone. Winnicott wrote about transitional space and transitional objects.

Transitional space is the territory provided for the child by the parent's attention and regard. The child senses that the parent has made her or his environment (kingdom!) safe (magical!) enough to go about the business (drama!) of moving on and ahead towards her or his truest (fullest!) self (expression!). Do you vaguely remember as a small child being completely absorbed in your own world—What's this hairy blob that huffs, huffs, huffs hot air?—at the same time that you were keenly aware that the hem of mother's skirt was no more than a long reach or quick scream away? That's it!

On the other hand, when there is not enough parental attention and regard, the infant worries too much about insufficient supplies of care. The child's fantastic journey towards the authentic self is sacrificed for a self that does whatever is necessary to secure parental nearness, and the safety and security it represents. The child's hand stays on the mother's skirt. The child thwarts the development of the "true self" for a "false self."

In the "good enough realm" of parental presence, the child becomes courageous enough to follow the hairy blob up the stairs without looking back. The child grows from greater to lesser dependence upon the parent through play and imagination. The child plays and imagines her or his self from a reality of symbiosis with the parent to realities illustrative of increasing separation and individuation.

In the transitional space between the child and parent are objects with which the child plays. Winnicott called these items transitional objects.[1] The transitional object is that which the child plays with, embraces, and clings to as she or he transitions from one developmental milestone to another. Winnicott wrote about the transitional object as the necessary companion to accompany the child through the hard and sometimes harsh realities of growing up.

The hairy blob is a transitional object. So are a thumb sucked, the favorite blanket or pillow demanded at bedtime, an imaginary friend, whom the mother or father comes to include in prayers, good night kisses and the like.

All of us had some form of transitional object. Many of us may remember them. At about age six, I had a football helmet. I painted number 19 on it, the number of Johnny Unitas, quarterback of the Baltimore Colts. I got through one difficult reality after another by putting on the helmet, going to the backyard and imagining myself throwing the winning touchdown pass to Jerry Richardson with time running out and 55,000 screaming fans cheering me on.

Priscilla and Wishbone's story reveals the truth that was at the heart of Winnicott's work with adults who

---

1. Winnicott, *Playing and Reality* (London:Tavistock, 1973), chapter 1.

came to him for psychotherapy, a truth he believed exists for all adults, whether they are in treatment or not: imaginative play in creative space continues beyond childhood.[2] We never really get over the need for transitional space and objects. At those times when we have to move through rough terrain, we are likely to clear transitional space for new transitional objects to appear, or for old ones to reappear. In transitional space, transitional objects bless us with a playful presence that allows us to persevere, to pass through and pass on. The most actualized and stable among us need a teddy bear every now and then.

During the initial years of the AIDS pandemic in Atlanta, when my colleagues and I weren't sure how to care, or if we were making any difference, I showed up at Symphony Hall on Friday night to play with whatever musical toys Robert Shaw put in the sandbox. Now, when I am having a particularly difficult day or week, I sometimes escape to the Impressionists Room at The Museum of Fine Arts in Boston and let my eyes rest upon Monet's Giverny or dance along with Renoir's prancing couple.

Priscilla and Wishbone's playfulness in the desert of the nursing home environment is that which we do well to create as weary souls who aim to get from here to there in what can be the desert of our daily lives. *Here* is a loved one lost, health taken away, a crummy relationship, a bent spirit, a desperate hour, a despairing situation, a difficult task, a hard job, a lost job, a virulent addiction. *There* is meaning, integrity, courage and hope.

Dancing around like a whirling dervish with the first peony of the season cradled in your arms. Digging pota-

---

2. Ann Belford Ulanov, *Finding Space: Winnicott, God, and Psychic Reality* (Louisville, Kentucky: Westminster John Knox Press, 2001), 14.

toes in late summer. Screaming "Yankees suck!" at Fenway Park in Boston. Playing Frisbee with a daughter or a dog. Finger painting on the floor. These *obligatos* of delight are not merely time off, entertainment, distractions, productive procrastination, or indulgence. They are sacraments on the path to the place of the skull.

Elisabeth Kubler-Ross left something out of her paradigm for trekking through the diminishments of body and spirit. Being a resourceful steward of our daily dying involves episodes of denial, anger, bargaining, depression, acceptance, and...*play*!

I still have my football helmet.

14 ॐ

Compassion Overload

*Jesus, perceiving in himself that power had gone forth
from him, immediately turned about in the crowd, and
said, "Who touched my garments?" And his disciples
said to him, "You see the crowd pressing around you,
and yet you say, 'Who touched me?'"*   Mark 5:30-31

Driving to work early one morning, I listened to a report on NPR about the high rate of burnout among caregivers in stressful situations. The interviewee said that
there had been a 100 percent turnover of clergy in
Columbine since the killing spree at the high school. A
third of the clergy had left ministry. A similar trend is
starting to emerge among caregivers in the greater New
York City area since September 11th.

The report took me back to an afternoon at the AIDS
hospice. I opened the door to the office of John, the director
of admissions, not thinking to knock first. Sitting in front of
John was a young man in a wheelchair. He was wasted to
the bone. His face expressed exhaustion and fear. His parents sat at his side, holding his hands. All four were weeping.

The next week, I saw John in the hall. I told him how sorry I was that I barged into his office, and how sad a scene it was. John didn't remember the experience.

In Columbine, after September 11th, at the AIDS hospice: the suffering can be so heavy for so long that the heart begins to nod off. The need for one's gentle and enduring presence seems so pressing that healers assume that there is not enough time to take a breather from the intensity of sadness and despair. We believe there is no right time to walk outside for an hour or away for a weekend to take the respite needed to remain aware of and available to self and others. Over-engaged hearts fall asleep on their feet.

Compassion overload is not confined to the professional caregiver. We are likely to care vigilantly, and without constraint, for the afflicted neighbor who is near enough to be called family or friend.

Jesus understood the path of enduring presence among the dispossessed. It took him up the mountain for a prayerful stillness, down the valley for engagement with and for the afflicted. The dynamic of solitude and engagement was one Jesus never forsook regardless of how inundated he was with the world's woes. The dynamic of mountaintop and valley equipped him with an immense and lasting capacity for attention. Attention so strong that Jesus, while rushing to heal Jairus's daughter, felt a woman's desperate touch while passing through a crowd so thick in need and number as to be suffocating. The prayerful balance of Jesus' compassionate life is a prescription for hearts so aroused they fall sleep.

So why do we leave the prescription in the medicine cabinet? We have a hard time saying "no" to another's need. We feel guilty for thinking about ourselves when others around us are suffering. We enjoy the exhilaration of being in the thick of things. We like to feel important and significant. We want to make a difference. We do not want to get left behind on the plentiful path to the place of the skull.

These reasons, while understandable and significant, are not legitimate. They equate solitude with time out and time away from the ones for whom we care.

Consider the possibility that solitude and engagement are two dimensions of the same experience—connection. In solitude on the mountain, Jesus concerned himself with the nature of his connection to "Abba." Through engagement in the valley, Jesus acted out the nature of his connection to "Abba."

The mother who spends day and night at the hospital with her child doesn't need a break as much as she needs space to contemplate what it means to be mother at the moment, and how that meaning is manifest in the immediate situation. Her hour in the hospital's atrium garden is not a "break." It is an important change in the climate of connection.

Persons who care beyond the pale don't burn out from overwork. They burn out from a lost sense of who they are, what they are called to be, in a relation that has been turned upside down in the environment of suffering. Burn out is less about lost energy and more about broken connection.

Craig crawled into bed with his wife, Alice, who was dying at the hospice. They slept together through the night. At the team meeting the next morning, the clinical director, upon reflecting on the experience, said, "That's what we aim for. We'll give the medications, change the diapers, watch the swelling, take the vitals so that a mate can be a mate instead of a practical nurse, which is what Craig would have had to be if Alice had stayed at home."

The clinical director's sentiment is similar to the one I felt for the wife who knelt with her husband at the altar rail last Sunday morning. Her "break" from an addicted husband is the twice-weekly Al Anon meetings she attends for refreshment. There she makes a way to remain aware of her commitment to be an enduring mate rather than an abiding enabler.

The prayerful balance of solitude and engagement in the care of those we love is more for the sake of relation than rest. That's important. For relation is what heals.

15 ❧

Out of the Darkness

*The light shines in the darkness, and the darkness did
not overcome it.*

John 1:5

Todd came to the pastoral counseling center on a mission. He said that he was depressed. He wanted to get on top of the blues before his marriage, which was six months away. Todd remarked that he had every reason to be happy, but often felt like he was walking up a steep hill in rain and windy weather on a chilly November day, shoes leaking, socks wet, and a full sack of potatoes on his back. Depression debilitates.

During the intake interview, I asked Todd to recall significant events in his life over the last few years. He named a graduation, a new law practice, meeting Angela, his fiancée. I noted that he had mentioned mostly good things. He paused for a few moments and then responded, "Well, my dad died two years ago, but the whole occasion was such a blur that I didn't even get a chance to experience his death."

Todd went on to say that his dad died a few weeks after his graduation from law school and a few days before the bar exam. He remembered rushing home to be with his mother, sailing through the funeral, hustling to get his father's doctor's office up for sale, and getting back to Atlanta before the exam. He said, "I didn't even have time to cry."

Todd and I spent the next few months unearthing the loss of his father, which had been buried under the ground of a life bustling with tying up lose ends, taking on heightened responsibilities, making new beginnings. The character of Todd's relation with his father was complex and conflicted, so his busyness was a convenient excuse not to deal with it. When we did, Todd slowly moved from depression to sadness. Sadness was Todd's healing.

Situational depression, depression whose roots are grounded more in experience than brain chemistry, is sadness stored in the top bin of the soul's icebox. A good portion of depression is frozen grief. Frozen grief often manifests as physical maladies. Studies have shown that the majority of persons who came to emergency rooms for treatment are dealing with unattended losses. Two of the psychiatrists I admire the most changed from family practice to psychiatry after discovering this among their patients.

I've learned over time and after many failed remedies for others and myself that a stolid spirit requires a great thawing of sorrow. The melting of depression is a slow, still process that demands gentle presence and enduring patience with one's self or another. It's not a "procedure" that can be put in the medicinal, spiritual, or psychotherapeutic microwave.

I remember a clinical pastoral education student in the hospice program, whose ministry with dying people I supervised. The student had been asked by a nurse manager to visit a depressed patient on the oncology ward. The student came to me frustrated by his inability to help the man.

The student had stopped by to visit the man every day for a week. Each time the student stuck his head in the door, the man would turn toward the window, curl up and not say a word. The student wanted to know how to "get" to the man, how to break through whatever barrier was constructed to keep him out.

I suggested that the student simply ask to come in, pull a chair up to the side of the bed, not too close, sit down and say nothing. Read, meditate, whatever. Stay for ten or fifteen minutes and then offer a "goodbye" and leave. Keep showing up that way for a few days.

After about five days, the man, after the student sat down, turned away from the window, said, "Hello," and asked the student where he was from. From that place, the pastoral relationship moved forward.

The man was waiting to see how much energy it was going to take to be connected to this "young fellow." How much was he, the patient, going to have to invest to keep the connection with the energetic chaplain sufficiently dramatic and poignant enough to meet the chaplain's needs and expectations? The patient wanted to know who was going to be taking care of whom. When the man determined that it was safe to open up without emptying out, he reached out.

The man handed the student bitterness towards others and the world that had wronged him. The student took the hand that was offered and resisted the temptation to do anything more. Over the course of a few weeks, the man's resentment and sullenness loosened, and loneliness and regret seeped into the pastoral relation. The latter feelings, less caustic and more convivial, created deeper connection. Company became the context for the man's "redemption and release." He died in relation, a foretaste of the feast to come.

The movement from depression to sadness is the

movement out of darkness into light on the trail of modest relation. A little light can slay a great darkness. A lot of light violates eyes that have become dilated in the dark.

16 ❧

The Closet's Cost

Peter turned and saw following them the disciple whom
Jesus loved, who had lain close to his breast at the sup-
per and had said, "Lord, who is it that is going to betray
you?" When Peter saw him, he said to Jesus, "Lord, what
about this man?" Jesus said to him, "If it is my will that
he remain until I come, what is that to you? Follow me!"

John 21:20-22

One of those closest to Jesus lived in the shadows of
John's Gospel. Who the beloved disciple was and why
his relationship with Jesus remained cryptic is a mystery.
Solving the mystery of their relation does not particularly interest me. Praying the mystery of their relation
has been a source of strength and encouragement.

Since my years at the center of the AIDS pandemic,
I have embraced prayerfully the relationship between
Jesus and the beloved disciple. Such prayerfulness helps
me abide amidst the harsh religious climate unready for
relational configurations that express abiding experiences of companioning. Those who care the most and

best for people dying from AIDS often are shut out from the church's ancient and essential ministrations of compassion and justice, shunned by those who were baptized and ordained to administer them.

Cameron had cared for Richard, his lover, for the last two years of Richard's life. The care was constant and demanding. When Richard was close to death, his mother took a leave of absence from her teaching job in rural North Carolina so that she could come and help with his care.

When Richard's mother arrived, Cameron quickly was displaced as the primary caregiver, and moved to the margins of Richard's life. Cameron was angry. Richard was chagrined but did not want to hurt his mother's feelings.

When Richard died, his mother informed Cameron that it would not be appropriate for him to attend the funeral back home. She said that their church would not understand. And she told Cameron that she had told the minister to tell the congregation that Richard had died from cancer. Cameron decided to attend anyway. He drove up with his best friend, Janice, who was also very close to Richard. Cameron and Janice sneaked into one of the rear pews just before the service began.

At the time of the eulogy, the minister preached platitudes about Richard that pretty much left out everything about Richard's life after he resigned as church organist to go off to college. Cameron bent down and shook his head. Janice stood up at the end of the sermon and said that she had some things she'd like to share about Richard.

Janice climbed into the pulpit. She began by saying that she didn't recognize the Richard the minister was talking about. She shared her memories of Richard's gift of friendship, his great contributions to the AIDS community in Atlanta, the preciousness of Richard and Cameron's relationship.

After the committal service at the grave in the church cemetery, Cameron and Janice quietly left. A week or so later, we had a memorial service in the side chapel of a gay-friendly church downtown. The chapel was packed with friends and representatives from many of the AIDS service organizations around town.

Janice's prophetic performance at Richard's funeral was every bit as powerful as the actions of Jeremiah, Micah, Habakkuk, and the likes. I'm not sure what good came to the congregation by Janice outing Richard, or to Richard's family. I do know how redemptive the outing was for Cameron and the Atlanta AIDS community.

We like to think that the present day atmosphere in the more progressive parishes no longer requires a prophetic voice like Janice's. We like to believe that cautious churches in conservative regions are more honest and open about gay relation than they were in Richard's day, the mid 1980's.

My take on the typical liberal parish regarding gay relation goes something like this: "Of course we accept them. Who are we to judge?" One doesn't have to listen too carefully to hear the inherent judgment in such an attitude.

My take on the typical liberal bishop regarding gay ordination goes something like this: "I'll ordain you. But be careful. Don't embarrass me or cause trouble." In other words, act straight.

The broad difference between Richard's childhood parish and, say, the urbane parish on the village green in the forward-thinking suburb north of the city is, sadly, one of degree rather than kind. Intolerance is to tolerance as grits are to polenta. Tolerance is to affirmation as grits are to golf balls. The closet door is cracked but hardly wide open. Our gay sisters and brothers live compromised lives among us.

There is work to do. Jesus and the beloved disciple might inspire us to get busier.

17 ✑

Listening to the Long Goodbye

The poor you always have with you, but you do not always have me.

                                                                John 12:8

Recently, my friend, Tom, gave his mother, Roberta, the gift of a good death.

Roberta was in her mid-eighties. Her heath was failing. During a battery of tests for Parkinson's disease in late spring, she was found to have lung cancer. Roberta's doctor wisely suggested that she not have surgery, because she would likely die of other causes before cancer killed her.

Later in the summer, Tom and his wife, Beth, took Roberta to Europe to visit close friends and favorite places. In the fall, he secured hospice services for Roberta, and drove from Boston to New York on the weekends to help with her care. When she took a turn for the worse in mid December, Tom arranged a Christmas party for close relatives. Roberta died peacefully on New Year's Day. Six months later, Tom and Beth invited family and friends to their mountain home to commit Roberta's ashes to the ground, at the foot of trees she loved.

When I told Tom that he had given his mother the gift of a good death, he responded by saying that he simply said the long goodbye.

Generous souls, such as Tom, are able and willing to say the long goodbye to those who are leaving for good, for a while, or for a different place and experience. Kindhearted folks, though, more often than not, have a difficult time hearing the long goodbye. We blush big time, literally and figuratively, when we are the recipients of regard.

When I worked in hospice, I served as a priest on the weekends in a parish in Lexington, Massachusetts. I assisted in liturgy and occasionally preached. When I decided to leave the hospice and return to full-time parish ministry, I announced to the parish that I would be leaving at the end of the summer to serve as a rector of another parish. The following Sunday, the senior warden approached me after Eucharist and said that the parish wanted to have a going-away party before I left. I said that such an offer was very kind and generous, but, since I had been very part-time, I did not feel like my leaving was a big deal. A party seemed unnecessary. I suggested possibly an acknowledgment of my leaving during the announcements before worship. The senior warden said, "Bill, you should pay more attention to the influence you have on people."

I understood the wisdom of the senior warden upon arriving at my new parish. I followed a rector who had been forced to leave after only a couple of years of ministry due to an irreconcilable conflict with the parish. He followed a rector who had served the parish for almost thirty years, and was adored, almost venerated.

The beloved rector gave a relatively short notice regarding his leaving, barely showed up at his reception at the time of his leaving, and dropped off the planet after his leaving. His leave-taking was so swift and cryptic that a few neighbors near the rectory thought he had been so shamefully fired that he had to leave in the dark of the night.

That the congregation was given little chance to say "goodbye" to their cherished leader exacerbated their difficult adjustment to the new rector, and made it hard for him to achieve fair footing. How can you be enraged at a gentle giant of a man who has loved you unselfishly for decades? Not so easily. You project it on the one who dares to take his place.

The venerated rector and I are in good company. Over the years of working in the community of the dying and bereaved, I noticed that those who cared the most for the dying and bereaved, and cared for them best—the nurses in particular—took bumpy roads out of the work place. They would abruptly leave, get entangled in controversies and quit, or drag themselves to going-away parties and be among the first to leave.

We are also in large company. Most of us know bighearted folks who have said, when relation is ending or changing, "Oh, it was nothing." Many of us have said it.

Those who give a lot usually have a hard time receiving a little. We assume that modesty is a virtue. Not so. Modesty protects the caring one from the loss of control that comes with being the beneficiary of regard. It preserves the power imbalance that favors the beneficent over the beneficiary. Deep gratitude cracks open, breaks through, and creates change in those upon whom it is showered. Grace is a great equalizer, a disrupter of patronizing relation.

Modesty also is a means of acting out our narcissistic tendencies. Acknowledgment given by the beneficiary in the same measure that care is received from the beneficent is acknowledgment completed. By avoiding direct acknowledgment of our beneficence by beneficiaries, we hold on to our significance. If we leave community with the balance of kindness and care weighted in our favor, a debt is owed. We have a tendency to enjoy having others in debt to us. No wonder Jesus threw in a parable or two about burning the books.

The opposite of the modest caregiver is not the proud do-gooder. Conceit is a rare condition among the generous. The opposite of modesty more likely is a deeper, more intimate connection to community requiring a greater investment and vulnerability of self than altruism. Once again, *agape* is safer, more comfortable than *eros*.

The best gift the one who departs can leave the person or communities she or he has cared for is the willingness to be openly thanked and acknowledged.

An experience in the community of the dying and bereaved offers a blueprint of mutual regard for the completion of relation.

Jeff was a friend to many, a leader in the AIDS community in the greater Boston area, and one of the initial planners of the city's first residential hospice facility. He decided to take his own life when his death from AIDS was imminent. He communicated his intentions early on to those closest to him. On the day of his death, he threw a party to remember. He thanked his friends and family members for being a part of his life. He offered intentional goodbyes to each of them, and let them say explicit and enthusiastic goodbyes to him. Regardless of the rightness or wrongness of his suicide, or the motivations for it, Jeff's well-orchestrated exit paid rich dividends to those left behind. His departure was a parting gift that his friends and family are still receiving.

18 ❧

A Heartful Helplessness

Hail Mary full of grace.

Luke 1:28

Twice a month, our hospice team gathered for what I called spiritual case conference. This was the time when we took off our "clinical hats" and sat together to share feelings about the one family on our caseload that presently was stirring up the most emotions for good or ill. Who was making us most sad or joyful, most angry or exhausted?

This particular morning, we were talking about Martha and her husband, Bob. The team was deeply drawn to Martha's presence, which had not been robbed of its richness even by the rigors of bone cancer. We were greatly touched by the bond between Martha and Bob, and Bob's dedication to her comfort and care. We talked about Martha's recent shift into a more active dying. Martha was spending more time in bed. She was resisting Bob's attempts to get her to eat and drink more, and sleep less.

Anna, a nurse on the hospice team, had grown particularly close to Martha, and Martha to her. They were of similar age, background, and interests. They had a special connection that was fashioned through many hours together. During the team's conversation about Martha shutting down and slowly slipping into her final days, Anna announced that she needed to excuse herself, that she was going to ride over to Martha's home with a walker she had set aside for her. Anna wanted to see if the walker might encourage Martha to get around a bit more.

Anna was a seasoned hospice nurse. She knew that the walker was not the answer, that there is no right answer to the question of how to keep Martha with us. Her aching heart had blinded her mind's eye.

By far, the hardest task for healers to perform is to remain relationally present amidst the profound sense of powerlessness that comes with not being able to abate or ease the diminishment, despair, or anxiety of dying persons and those who love them. The healer's greatest challenge is to stay still, feet firmly grounded and heart wide open, during the hurricane of dying, the strongest winds being those of the healer's inadequacy to make things well.

Scripture gives testimony to both heroic and not so heroic helplessness amidst the hurricane of dying. First, a story about those for whom the gusts of inadequacy were too strong, Jesus' closest friends.

On the eve of his death, Jesus headed to the garden of Gethsemane. There he would groan through his greatest despair and fears about his pending execution. He would plead for reprieve from, and finally succumb to, divine love's uncompromising end. Jesus asked his closest friends to come with him. Once there, Jesus asked them simply to wait with him as he prayed: "Then Jesus went with them to a place called Gethsemane, and he said to his disciples, 'Sit here, while I go yonder and pray.' And taking with him Peter and the two sons of Zebedee, he began to be sorrowful and troubled."[1]

The disciples fell asleep. Not once but three times: "And he came to the disciples and found them sleeping; and he said to Peter, 'So, could you not watch with me one hour? Watch and pray that you may not enter into temptation; the spirit indeed is willing, but the flesh is weak.'"[2]

I imagine that Peter, James and John were so anxious about not being able to do something to save or salve their friend and teacher that they checked out through sleep. At least through sleep they did not impede his path. The scene would have been worse if they had checked out wide-awake, with the busyness of word and deed: "Don't worry, we'll get through this." "They'll have to take me first." "Let's go back to the hills for a few more days and think this through."

And then there is Mary, the mother of Jesus, whose whole life seemed to be one of heroic helplessness[3] amidst a succession of vicious hurricanes of dying both this side of and at the grave. To Gabriel's absurd pronouncement of an impregnation that would impugn her character if true and indict her sanity if shared, she said, in so many words, "So be it."[4] Soon after giving birth, when shepherds told her that the baby belonged not to her but eternity, she "kept all these things, pondering

---

1. Matthew 26:36-37.
2. Matthew 26:40-41.
3. I first heard the term, heroic helplessness, from grief therapist, Shirley Holzer Jeffrey.
4. Luke 1:38.

them in her heart."[5] When her adolescent child ran away to church for three days, and, when found, responded to her anxiety with veiled sarcasm, it was enough for her not to understand.[6] When her son was executed in the cruelest fashion, she stayed near.[7]

Something eternal and heavenly flows from the healer, who, like Mary, is able to offer heroic helplessness amidst and at the side of those suffering the severest compromises and negations. For that which usually and soon enough issues from heroic helplessness is heartful helplessness.

A healer's helplessness at not being able to make dying and bereaved persons well, which she or he heroically bears, is revealed as the same helplessness dying and bereaved persons suffer at the hand of their disease and loss. The healer realizes that the most precious gift she or he has to give to the dying and bereaved is the helplessness she or he bears in the face of not being able to make them well. The healer's helplessness becomes an empathic bond. The bond is strong enough to erase the distinctions between the one who gives care and the one who receives it. Distinctions such as well and sick, caregiver and patient, living and dying dissolve. *Powerlessness with* is transposed to *power between*.

Anna never made it to Martha's home with the walker. When Anna announced her departure from the spiritual case conference, one of the nurse's aids stood up, walked over to Anna, gave her a big hug, and acknowledged how hard it must be to see Martha start to let go. Anna sat down and cried. Those closest to Anna put their helpless arms around her. It was a heartful moment pregnant with healing.

---

5. Luke 2:20.
6. Luke 2:48-51.
7. John 19:25.

When Anna did make it to Martha's later in the afternoon, she arrived as a fellow struggler. Furthermore, as the nurse's aid had been to her, so could she now be present to Bob in a way that would help him find a heroic helplessness beside Martha and possibly a heartful helplessness to offer and share with her.

Anna's journey is ours. When our loved ones and friends are hurting, our inability to lighten their load, brighten their spirits, improve their situation is too hard to endure. So, we fall asleep at their side, like Jesus' friends, by getting busy in and about their lives.

I can spend most of a day as a priest offering much heroic helplessness and an episode or two of heartful helplessness. When I get home at the end of the day and discover that my mate has had a terrible day concerning this or that, I am the first to serve up a solution. If I'm lucky, I catch myself. Sometimes it takes the inevitable failure of my zealous efforts to make well, registered by my mate's indifference during my good advice, for me to remember Mary.

We all do well to carry a symbolic rosary in our chest pocket on the plentiful path to the place of the skull. When a dear one's suffering draws near, we can put a hand to our chest, clutch Mary, and stay still long enough to have the other hand of our own suffering involuntarily reach out and touch the neighbor. The sacrament of shared suffering is celebrated.

19 ☙

Scarcity and Abundance

Judas Iscariot, one of his disciples (he who was to betray him), said, "Why was this ointment not sold for three hundred denarii and given to the poor?" Jesus said, "Let her alone, let her keep it for the day of my burial."

John 12:4-5, 7

Recently, I read about the Jewish ritual of *Tahara*, the preparation of the dead for burial, which dates from six-teenth-century Poland.[1] Those who perform the ritual, the *Chevra Kadisha*, enter the room, call the corpse by its Hebrew name, and ask pardon for any indignity they may visit on it as they work. The washing is replete with smell, fluids, and dead weight. The workers wash the skin, swab the ears, comb the hair, and clean the nails. Only the por-

---

1.Catherine Madsen, "Love Songs to the Dead: The Liturgical Voice as Mentor and Reminder," a paper presented, in 1998, at the consultation of *The Association for Religion and Intellectual Life*. The paper can be read on the internet at http://www.crosscurrents.org/madsen.htm.

tion of the body being washed is uncovered; it is as if the corpse was still alive, able to feel humiliation.[2]

While bathing the body, the *Chevra Kadisha* sings verses from the Song of Songs, chapter 5, verses 11-15:

> His head is the finest gold; his locks are wavy, black as a raven. His eyes are like doves beside springs of water, bathed in milk, fitly set. His cheeks are like beds of spices, yielding fragrance. His lips are lilies, distilling liquid myrrh. His arms are rounded gold, set with jewels. His body is ivory work, encrusted with sapphires. His legs are alabaster columns, set upon bases of gold. His appearance is like Lebanon, choice as the cedars.

The Jewish heart sings abundantly in death's scarce chambers. The irony is understandable in light of the Jewish heart's capacity not to connect death with the dearth of existence. The Jewish relation to death, both physical and existential, is more about abundance than scarcity. Death is more a profusion of sadness, yearning, embracing, and connecting than it is a diminishment.

That the *Chevra Kadisha* sings sumptuously among those whom our culture tellingly calls "stiffs" is instructive for a society whose postmodern preoccupation with death is best characterized as cosmic sting. The Jewish heart teaches us that the desert of death is something to which to be relationally present with immense curiosity, deep respect, and great expectation rather than something to be passed through, towards an eternal *Vegas*, with a functional cooling system and full tank of gas. Death is a desert that teems with life. Yet, like the desert around Phoenix, the desert of death requires our time and attention to reveal her bounty.

We have squandered Jewish wisdom about death. Our

---

2. Ibid.

culture's disposition towards death as that which ends and empties life, permeates the institutions that shape our lives. Our body politic is one of scarcity, irrespective of the immense abundance we enjoy. The aim and attitude of government, corporations, religious bodies, and families reflect a fear of death by striving to persevere and prosper against the uncertainties and diminishments of life. The greater our abundance the more heightened is our sensitivity to scarcity. Logic suggests that those who have the most might hoard the least, those who have the least might hoard the most. The logic is lost on us.

The fear of death that fashions a politic of scarcity tempts us to worship preservation and prosperity. A big slice of our lives is designed to answer a couple of key questions from our cultural catechism: What will we make of the opportunities that have been handed down to us from our past? What will we pass on to others in the future? The measure of how well we are answering these questions in the present moment has to do with the material insurance and security we've garnered to date. Sure, there are other values operative in our society that have to do with education, religion, patriotism, community, and service. Yet, these values are of secondary concern, and often are in the service of the cultural catechesis.

My daughter and son are now in high school. It seems as if the entire curricular and extra-curricular emphases are on where their mother and I will send the first college tuition check. Where the check is sent suggests the size of their first position and paycheck. The emphases are not necessarily the ones they've chosen. Our generation cooked up the deal, as the generation before us cooked up ours.

The cultural catechism has a prominent place on the shelf of mainline faith. Take, for instance, the envy of every parish—endowment (a curse in disguise). Endowed parishes sweat bullets trying to make the best out of the beneficence of others. They are slower than poorer parishes to register their own liberality as the litmus test of solvency. Add external factors such as market performance to the mix, and you get a sufficient parish that administrates against, and moans about, scarcity.

On the other hand, parishes that do not have enough money in the bank to cover expenses six months out wonder more than worry about material matters. Insufficient parishes administrate in anticipation of abundance bubbling up from the pool of their shared scarcity. They find the wherewithal to carry on through the means of grace cited by Martin Luther in The Smalcald Articles: "...the mutual conversation and consolation of the [sisters and] brothers."[3] Luther considered this means of grace to be both as essential and significant as Word and Sacrament.

We learn from the *Chevra Kadisha* to embrace scarcity, not to shield and protect ourselves from, nor organize ourselves around, it. By their examples, they invite us to perform an act of faith, to squeeze the paucity of existence *as if* there is abundant life therein. To sing the Song of Songs over the scarcity of our lives, over the scarcity that permeates a broken world, is to take an audacious, some would say absurd, leap. We are trusting that we will find the blessed richness of being by choosing not to defend against the daily deaths this side of, at, and beyond the graves that pocket life-the-way-it-really-is. We are trusting that abundant life abounds amidst the scarcity of life. I have found such faith not to be ill placed.

The key to sustaining our faith is to remember that the *Chevra Kadisha* is a choir of sorts—companions in concert. There are no lone rangers on the plentiful path to the place of the skull.

---

3. Theodore G. Tappert, et. al., eds., *The Book of Concord* (Philadelphia: Fortress Press, 1959), 303.

20 🙌

Inspiriting Institutions

Jesus said to them, "Have you never read in the scrip-
tures: 'The very stone that the builders rejected has be-
come the head of the corner; this was the Lord's doing,
and it is marvelous in our eyes'?"   Matthew 21: 442

I have an entrepreneur friend with a big heart; his en-
terprising endeavors have made a difference for the good.

Recently, my friend's mother died. In response to his
comment that the hospice care she received was on the
whole mediocre, I noted that the hands of hospice have
been tied by American-style medicine. Passionate presence with dying persons and those who love them is embedded in managed care protocols and profit margins.
Hospices barely get by. In fact, in 1999 more hospice
programs went out of business than were started. That
trend continues.

My friend became interested in doing something
about the hospice bind. He saw an opportunity to merge
expertise and money to free hospice's hands, if only a little. He was determined to devise a model program that

would work in and around the health care system, and attract investors interested in more than the bottom line. For the task, he put together a team comprised of both the best practitioners and policy makers in the hospice and health care worlds.

After several months of earnest effort, my friend decided that the most reasonable and wise decision would be to pass up the opportunity. Most of the fiscally sound programs investigated were dependent more upon economy of scale than quality of care. The people who ran them were not exactly the kind of folks with whom he would want to spend a casual Friday evening. There was not a way to make the reimbursement streams supply enough resources to support the kind of program that would have worked for his mother, and, by extension, most persons and families facing terminal illness. The gathered experts suggested that the breakthrough would come when the present health care system imploded. My friend was not interested in beginning a venture by waiting to bend down and pick up broken pieces.

The history of hospice's heart disease spans a mere quarter of a century. Hospice began in the mid 1970s through the zealous efforts of a handful of people at Yale New Haven Hospital. I jumped on board early, in 1975. A member of the church I served as an intern from Yale Divinity School invited me to accompany him to visit a cancer patient he regularly saw as a volunteer of the first hospice program in the nation.

I was smitten. I joined the fledgling movement by participating in hospice programs in the cities where I served parishes. I was a patient care volunteer, board member, and, eventually, an active participant in the dialog concerning the future of hospice in America.

Our dream was that hospice would go out of business by the turn of the century. Hospice would have humanized the medical world's care of dying persons and those who love them to a degree that hospice as a separate delivery system would be superfluous.

Hospice began as a fit and trim justice-making movement. It has become a compassionate institution with a weight problem.

Sound familiar? It is the predominant plot of most religions. Spirited movements for justice turn to codified institutions that mirror the values and norms of the cultures in which they exist.

Take, for instance, the Christian story. Jesus, an itinerant Jewish peasant who was bigger than his creeds, is martyred. From that martyrdom, a movement began. Of that martyrdom, much has been made. Over time, that movement reflects less and less of its original spirit and increasingly manifests the conventions—and sanctifies the causes—of city hall and the chamber of commerce.

The character of Brother Jesus has been buried in the Corporation of Jesus Christ. A movement of unmodified justice has become an institution of measured compassion. A bold cornerstone has been chiseled into a benign crown.

My hope for the church is built on the fact that cornerstone and crown are from the same rock. The church always has been, and continues to survive as, the alchemy of movement and institution. The church's legitimacy is linked to a capacity to keep reforming herself from the inside out. The true church is embedded in the historical church, but not to be distinguished from it, as Luther liked to say.

Now and then, the embeddedness of Brother Jesus in the Body of Christ must become the burr under the saddle of ecclesial stasis. At times, the church is called to rise to the occasion. Here and there, it is incumbent upon those who claim to be Christian to invite the One who is bigger than the creeds about him to pull up to the table of a church that is smaller than her avowed beliefs. Social crisis and shifting societal sands demand that the church conference with Brother Jesus, the pre-Christian Jew, who has us tackle the most difficult things in a post-Christian world.

Brother Jesus brings to the table such matters as war with Iraq, same sex unions, America's drive for global dominance, clergy sexual abuse, the corporations represented in our denomination and parish investment portfolios, gay ordination, the homeless people on our church doorsteps, global warming, the seven different and competing steeples within a two minute walk, as well as the relational dynamics these issues represent—authority, power, abuse, diversity, inclusivity, greed, vulnerability, and peace.

With Brother Jesus as consultant, the risk of reaching unsettling conclusions and actions is real.

Following Brother Jesus within the Church of Jesus Christ and into a broken world means putting ourselves in an expendable position. The surest confidence we have to go forward as crucifiable people flows from the cool spring of our pooled susceptibility to a godly sense of things.

Conclusion
"Break forth, O beauteous heavenly light, and usher in the morning"

He descended into Hell.

The Apostles' Creed

Jesse could really warm a heart. An old timer at the AIDS clinic, Jesse embraced the hospital-green, basement-dampened corridor that was the waiting room and squeezed laughter out of it. One morning he would be found in front of the television loudly taking sides with one of Oprah's guests, "Honey, let your sister have the old bastard." Another afternoon, he would present a basket of brightly colored condoms to a grandmother, instructing her to chose one to give to her grandson when he emerged from the treatment rooms, suggesting that he may need something fun to think about.

When Jesse wasn't making mirth, he might be found manufacturing courage by offering a heartening word to those showing up for their first, scary appointments. Or, he would boast to someone with the big, black splotches that come with AIDS-related Kaposi's sarcoma that their lesions looked like specks compared to the ones he used to wear: "Sugar, I caused a dalmatian to drop dead of envy."

When Jesse's symptoms finally took hold, he was referred to our hospice program. Among the hospice community, the joy of his presence grew in proportion to his dying. The volunteer assigned to him, a medical student, couldn't get enough of his company. She told me that her time with Jesse, like no other part of her training, had confirmed her decision to be a doctor. At the clinical team meetings, Jesse's case, when it came up, usually took too much time. He was a trill of light in a symphony of darkness, which we liked to play repeatedly.

I sometimes felt that a few of the people we cared for would actually dupe death, outlast, explode, or extinguish it. Jesse was one of those I imagined might pull it off. But he did not. Furthermore, his dying painted a burning question mark across the hospice team's heart, the first brush stroke of which was made at the team meeting a few weeks before Jesse's death.

The social worker presented Jesse's plans for his dying. He would go back to his rural, South Georgia home, with the stipulation from his mom and dad that he meet two conditions. Once there, he would be baptized in the conservative church of his childhood in order to cover the sins of what his family considered, and he was now calling, a promiscuous life. He would be buried in straight clothes, a suit, something he did not own, being the rather extravagant and quite glamorous drag queen that he was.

The hospice team was confused and miffed. There was nothing in Jesse's life among us that needed redeeming; indeed, on more than one occasion, the grace of his presence had saved us from gloom. And, Jesse was loved by enough people in Atlanta to ensure a comfortable death, with lots of company, within the confines of his authentic self. We wondered if Jesse had experienced a sincere change of heart, or whether he was morphing back to the manners of his clan in order to have a bed among them in which to die. We would never know.

I spent a good part of my life as a Lutheran. Lutherans hang on, with pride, to a section of the Apostles' Creed at which most Christians look askance, the part that says: "He descended into Hell." Lutherans don't worry too much about the sentence's lack of biblical weight. There is just too much good grace to be had in the image of Jesus spending Holy Saturday storming Hell, springing the locks on the cells in which every alienated person has been imprisoned along with their isolating experiences and acts of estrangement.

I like to ponder prayerfully the fate of Jesse's final days in a Lutheran sort of way: Jesse, on the deathbed of his roots, with more grace than any code could contain. Jesse's precious self persisting against clan's praises of and pronouncements about the accouterment of his deathbed conversion. Jesse, spending the Holy Saturday of his end time grabbing a good acre or two for heaven's reign in one of Hell's righteous regions.

I like to imagine Jesse cryptically cleansing the baptism pool into which he was dunked to de-breed what the deacons decried as dirtiness. I like to imagine Jesse showing up on his parents' terms as a final gift to them, the offering of their son, knowing, as he did, that they would never "get" the way he really was.

Whatever the character of his incarnations of grace in "God's country," I know there were manifestations of some degree and kind. The Jesse we knew—his spirit formed more fully in the community occasioned by his illness—would make a difference in the darkness.

His spirit did form more fully in that community. The sacrament of shared suffering strengthened Jesse for what I imagined to be his descent into Hell.

There is an apropos line from Eucharistic Prayer C in *The Book of Common Prayer:* "Deliver us from the presumption of coming to this Table for solace only, and not for strength; for pardon only, and not for renewal."

The sacrament of shared suffering, which we may partake of in the midst of our many deaths and bereavements of daily life, strengthens us for storming Hell on the bleak Holy Saturdays of our existence. We have been empowered by the tie that binds—our mutual woes—to liberate others and ourselves from the lowest regions of our lived experience.

The sacrament of shared suffering helps shape a spiritual physique that is firm enough to free us from the prisons of a past we have eluded, escaped, or become ensconced in, a present by which we feel stained, a future we do not feel emancipated enough to engage. I know that the stories I have shared with you throughout these pages, many of which I was a part of, encourage and equip me to visit hurtful neighborhoods in the complex city of my life in relation, and to find some healing therein.

There is water in the wastelands. Drink.